AF829343

Insurance Market Integration in the European Union

This book offers an in-depth analysis of the mechanisms of insurance market integration and measures the degrees of this integration. It examines the operation of the EU single financial market and, against this backdrop, the regulation relating to the insurance market. In addition, the book focuses on the specificity and determinants of international insurance market development and the issues with assimilation set against other financial market segments such as money market, credit-deposit and bond and equity. It discusses the advantages and disadvantages of insurance market integration on an international scale.

The authors propose a unique approach to the subject in the context of the EU and particularly in relation to the European area. They also apply new measures of insurance market integration in the EU in practice through the use of statistical data and implementation of econometric modeling. Further, they investigate how the financial and fiscal crisis has affected the insurance market in EU countries and the impact of European Central Bank monetary policy on the degrees of integration in the European area during and after the financial crisis.

This book will find an audience among academics and researchers in the fields of international economics and finance and applied, financial and growth economics.

Sławomir Ireneusz Bukowski is a full professor of economics and finance and rector at Kazimierz Pulaski University of Technology and Humanities, Radom, Poland.

Marzanna Barbara Lament is associate professor of finance and accounting in the Faculty of Economics and Finance, Kazimierz Pulaski University of Technology and Humanities, Radom, Poland.

Banking, Money and International Finance

26 Global Stock Market Development
Quantitative and Behavioural Analysis
Marcin Kalinowski

27 The Digitalization of Financial Markets
The Socioeconomic Impact of Financial Technologies
Edited by Adam Marszk and Ewa Lechman

28 The Digital Disruption of Financial Services
International Perspectives
Edited by Ewa Lechman and Adam Marszk

29 The Economics and Finance of Commodity Price Shocks
Mikidadu Mohammed

30 Digital Finance and the Future of the Global Financial System
Disruption and Innovation in Financial Services
Edited by Lech Gąsiorkiewicz and Jan Monkiewicz

31 Artificial Intelligence and Big Data for Financial Risk Management
Intelligent Applications
Edited by Noura Metawa, M. Kabir Hassan and Saad Metawa

32 The Role of Crises in Shaping Financial Systems
From the Global Financial Crisis to COVID-19
Małgorzata Iwanicz-Drozdowska, Elżbieta Malinowska-Misiąg, Piotr Mielus, Paweł Smaga, and Bartosz Witkowski

33 Insurance Market Integration in the European Union
Sławomir Ireneusz Bukowski and Marzanna Barbara Lament

For more information about this series, please visit: www.routledge.com/series/BMIF

Insurance Market Integration in the European Union

Sławomir Ireneusz Bukowski
and Marzanna Barbara Lament

Routledge
Taylor & Francis Group
LONDON AND NEW YORK

First published 2023
by Routledge
4 Park Square, Milton Park, Abingdon, Oxon OX14 4RN

and by Routledge
605 Third Avenue, New York, NY 10158

Routledge is an imprint of the Taylor & Francis Group, an informa business

© 2023 Sławomir Ireneusz Bukowski and Marzanna Barbara Lament

The right of Sławomir Ireneusz Bukowski and Marzanna Barbara Lament to be identified as authors of this work has been asserted in accordance with sections 77 and 78 of the Copyright, Designs and Patents Act 1988.

All rights reserved. No part of this book may be reprinted or reproduced or utilised in any form or by any electronic, mechanical, or other means, now known or hereafter invented, including photocopying and recording, or in any information storage or retrieval system, without permission in writing from the publishers.

Trademark notice: Product or corporate names may be trademarks or registered trademarks, and are used only for identification and explanation without intent to infringe.

British Library Cataloguing-in-Publication Data
A catalogue record for this book is available from the British Library

Library of Congress Cataloging-in-Publication Data
Names: Bukowski, Sławomir, author. | Lament, Marzanna Barbara, author.
Title: Insurance market integration in the European Union / Sławomir Ireneusz Bukowski and Marzanna Barbara Lament.
Description: 1 Edition. | New York, NY : Routledge, 2023. | Series: Banking, money and international finance | Includes bibliographical references and index.
Identifiers: LCCN 2022020135 (print) | LCCN 2022020136 (ebook) | ISBN 9781032131184 (hardback) | ISBN 9781032131207 (paperback) | ISBN 9781003227762 (ebook)
Subjects: LCSH: Insurance--European Union countries.
Classification: LCC HG8592 .B85 2023 (print) | LCC HG8592 (ebook) | DDC 368/.94--dc23/eng/20220718
LC record available at https://lccn.loc.gov/2022020135
LC ebook record available at https://lccn.loc.gov/2022020136

ISBN: 978-1-032-13118-4 (hbk)
ISBN: 978-1-032-13120-7 (pbk)
ISBN: 978-1-003-22776-2 (ebk)

DOI: 10.4324/9781003227762

Typeset in Times New Roman
by KnowledgeWorks Global Ltd.

To
Olivier Leon and Leon Patrick Bukowski

and

Marta Alicja Kunecka and Michał Adam Kunecki,
representatives of the new generation

Contents

Figures

Tables

About the authors

Sławomir Ireneusz Bukowski is a full professor (Titr.) of economics and finance, PhD, DSc, rector at Kazimierz Pulaski University of Technology and Humanities in Radom, Poland and head of the Department of International Business and Finance within the structure of the Faculty of Economics and Finance in Kazimierz Pulaski University of Technology and Humanities in Radom, Poland. He is the author of more than 190 scientific publications (among them 6 books, numerous papers in English, Polish and Russian and editor of 6 books), the author and co-author of 150 scientific reports and author of expert opinions for business. He has given lectures at universities in Belgium, France, Germany, Great Britain, Greece, Italy, Portugal, Russia, Slovakia, Spain and Turkey. He is a member of the Polish Economic Association, Polish Society of Banking & Finance, American Economic Association, Society for the Study of Emerging Markets, and Association for Comparative Economic Studies. His main scientific interests include: international economics, financial economics, financial markets, financial integration, economic growth theory and policy, and implementation of quantitative methods in research in the previously mentioned fields.

Marzanna Barbara Lament is an associate professor of finance and accounting, PhD, DSc, dean of the Faculty of Economics and Finance, Kazimierz Pulaski University of Technology and Humanities in Radom, Poland. She has given lectures in accounting and finance at the Universidá da Beira Interior in Covilha (Portugal), Technological Educational Institute of Epirus (Greece) and Matej Bel University (Slovakia), and during postgraduate studies in the fields of insurance and risk management in the financial institution organised by Warsaw School of Economics and Academy of Finance, Warsaw, Poland. She is a member of the Capital Banking Newspaper competition, A Friendly Insurance Company. Her main research interests include: solvency of insurance companies, information systems of insurance company accounting and non-financial reporting of insurance companies. She has authored more than 100 research publications.

Preface

International integration of financial markets is already highly advanced on a global, regional scale and, in particular, in the Euro area. Trade liberalisation and liberalisation of the flow of manufacturing factors, including capital flows and growing internationalisation, information, communication technology progress and a knowledge-based economy, are at the heart of the said integration.

Up until now, we have relatively good definitions, mechanisms, indicators and know-how to analyse financial market integration. But generally, we are concerned with the following segments: money markets, credit and deposit markets and capital markets (stocks and bonds markets). Nobody deals with the insurance market integration. Of course from a legal point of view in the EU, we have regulations common for all member countries (for example, one licence principle, solvency II, etc.), but from economic and financial points of view, up until now there is no concept of that integration and measures. Research on a single insurance market was carried out by many researchers whose research results are quoted in this book. However, they did not propose measures to assess the degrees of integration of insurance markets.

The aim of this book is to answer the following question: what is the mechanism of insurance market integration and measures of the degrees of this integration?

Our hypothesis is as follows: integration of insurance markets exists and we can find the proper measures of the degrees of that integration.

We have created and proposed measures of the degrees of insurance markets.

In search of answers to the formulated research question and in order to verify the research hypothesis, literature on the subject and statistical data of insurance markets were analysed.

We have also investigated the influence of the monetary policy (QE) on the insurance market and degrees of insurance market integration.

The book consists of five chapters.

Chapter 1 presents the problems of general characteristics of the single financial market in the EU. The authors analyse the institutions and its functions in the development of a single financial market, especially legal regulations concerning all segments of a financial market and its economic results.

In Chapter 2, the main segments of financial market specificities and determinants of financial market development are analysed. A very important part of this chapter is the analysis of the development of insurance markets segments. The following part concerns the econometric analysis of the impact of determinants on the development of insurance markets in the EU and also the impact of insurance market development on economic growth in the EU.

Chapter 3 discusses background for the following chapters. The authors present the main definitions, principles and fundamentals of the measures concerning the degree of integration of money markets, loan and deposit markets, bond markets and equity markets on an international scale in short and synthetic forms. They also present the synthetically empirical degree of financial market integration in the EU. The analysis allows them to formulate conclusions concerning the construction of insurance market degree measures.

In Chapter 4, the main differences between the insurance market and the other financial markets are presented. The authors define insurance market integration and present the main measures concerning the degree of insurance market integration. An important part of this chapter concerns the advantages and disadvantages of international insurance market integration.

Chapter 5 is empirical. The authors present the results of their own research concerning insurance market integration in the EU (1999–2019). First, they present the results of their research concerning the degree of insurance integration in the Euro area and econometric analysis of the dependency between insurance market integration and economic growth in the EU, especially in the Euro area (1999–2019). After, they analyse the impact of the financial crisis (2008–2012) on insurance market integration in the Euro area. Also important to discuss is the impact of monetary policy (quantitative easing) on the Euro area in the degrees of insurance market integration from 2008–2019.

This book is a result of many years of research carried out at Kazimierz Pulaski University of Technology and Humanities in Radom in the Faculty of Economics and Finance. It summarises a crucial stage in the authors' common research.

Sławomir Ireneusz Bukowski and Marzanna Barbara Lament
Radom, Poland, 2022

1 Single financial market in the EU

Financial market and its segments

The financial market is a key market in an economy, connected with the market of products, services and labour through supply-demand and price feedbacks. It is an area where short-, medium- and long-term financial transactions are closed, on the one hand, and a mechanism for the mobilisation of short- and long-term capitals and their allocation to the financing of investment undertakings is developed, on the other.

Financial instruments, incorporating capital, are traded in the financial market. A financial instrument is a contract (agreement) between two parties that governs their mutual financial dependence.

The financial market has its infrastructure, a network of links among banks, investment fund societies, insurance companies and stock exchanges. Financial institutions, enterprises, households and the state are the participants in the financial market. They both supply financial capitals and use them at a percentage price.

The financial market fulfils important functions in the economy. First, it's a mechanism of capital mobilisation for investment purposes, its allocation and conversion of the financial into production capital. Second, it sets capitals' pricing and allows for estimating investment risk, which is the starting point for investment decisions. Third, it enhances the motivational role of profits in enterprises and allows for their valuation. Fourth, it provides the economy with liquidity, which means that any money requirements of firms are met. In addition, the financial market plays a major role in the absorption of effects of economic shocks.

The financial market institutions comprise the legal system governing capital trade, the institutions of state financial supervision, financial intermediaries and financial instrument exchanges.

The legal system governing capital trade lays down the rules of public and non-public trade in capital (financial instruments), "the rules of the game" for participants in this trade. It is designed to ensure the security of capital trade, including that of financial investments. The distinction between the public and non-public trade in financial instruments is notional. The usual criterion

DOI: 10.4324/9781003227762-1

denotes the number of parties to which a sale of financial instruments is offered. The public trade in financial instruments is normally subject to special supervision by dedicated state institutions and to special requirements to be met by those issuing the instruments with regard to the presentation of business information, financial collateral, method of issue, etc.

The financial market's operation and conformity to the regulations of capital trade are supervised by dedicated state institutions like banking, insurance, pension fund supervisory authorities, and the securities and exchange commission. Some countries integrate these institutions of financial supervision.

These are intermediaries capable of operating in the financial market: universal, commercial and investment banks, societies of mutual investment funds (also known as fiduciary or investment funds), insurance companies, quasi-bank financial institutions (savings and credit unions, mutual benefit societies and credit cooperatives) and brokerage houses.

Financial instrument exchanges are formal markets, which means that financial instruments are traded there according to fixed rules, at fixed times and locations. The literature distinguishes a range of exchange types depending on what is traded, including stock (shares, bonds and derivative instruments), commodity (including term commodity), insurance, freight and energy exchanges. Given the subject matter of this book, we shall focus on stock exchanges.

The financial market's structure can be described with a variety of criteria. In respect of the geographical extent, a domestic and international market can be distinguished. Moreover, local (national or foreign) markets, where financial transactions of a national or regional scope are carried out, and international markets, where entities from different countries enter into transactions, can be recognised. Based on the time horizon of investments, short- and long-term capital markets can be found, with capitals invested for up to a year for purposes not yet ultimately determined by investors in the former. In the latter markets, the time horizon of financial investments is longer than a year. In line with this division, it would be hard to clearly categorise the market of derivative instruments inside the structure of long-term capital market since its transactions may be both short- and medium-term. This market is commonly treated separately, therefore.

Cash and credit-deposit instruments (of a time horizon below a year) are traded in the short-term capital market. These include bank and interbank deposits, treasury bills, commercial bills (or debt securities), deposit certificates, bills of exchange, cheques, short-term bank credits, loans, repo and reverse repo transactions, banker acceptance drafts and currencies.

It has already been mentioned that the time horizon of investments in this market is below a year and the ultimate purpose of capitals is not yet determined.

Capitals are supplied to this market from excess cash of enterprises, financial institutions, public finance sector institutions, household savings and the resources of mutual investment funds and of insurance companies. The capitals are demanded, however, by banks and other financial institutions, enterprises needing to improve their financial liquidity and households. Ensuring liquidity in the economy is the key function of this market.

Instruments expressing capital ownership or debt are transacted in long-term capital markets (or capital markets), with the time horizon of investments above a year. The instruments in this market encompass shares, treasury, local and corporate bonds, investment certificates and depositary receipts.

Capitals are supplied to this market from undistributed profits of enterprises, banks and other financial institutions, household savings, deposits of mutual investment funds, insurance companies and pension funds. The demand for capital, however, is represented by new enterprises, recent but expanding enterprises, banks and financial institutions, mutual investment funds, insurance companies, the state and households.

The capital market can be divided into the primary market, where new securities are sold directly by issuers, and the secondary market, where securities are offered by entities other than their issuers.

The secondary market is the domain of financial instrument exchanges and regulated off-exchange markets.

The supply of financial instruments to the primary market is determined by the following factors: the willingness of enterprises to invest, the availability of alternative methods of business financing and the state's demand for loan budget revenue. The demand for financial instruments in the primary market, in turn, arises from the rate of internal savings in the economy, saving habits of the public and the organisation of the capital market.

The secondary demand for and supply of financial instruments are results of varying needs and preferences of the entities that have already invested their savings in the instruments and of their willingness to invest capital in financial instruments that have traded for some time.

According to the organisation, exchange and off-exchange markets are distinguished.

The unique nature of financial instruments is a major criterion of classifying the segments of the financial market. A reasonable and interesting division is suggested by W. Dębski (2003, p. 21). Accordingly, the financial market consists of the monetary market (interbank deposits, repo and reverse repo transactions, treasury bills, commercial papers, certificates of deposits and bills), deposit and credit market (bank deposits, bank loans and credits), capital market (shares, treasury bonds, municipal bonds, corporate bonds, investment certificates and deposit receipts), currency market (currencies) and the market of derivative instruments (derivatives) (forwards, futures, options, swaps, etc.). The insurance market, where insurance policies and guarantees are the instruments, will extend this classification. It needs to be remembered, though any classification is a considerable simplification of reality. Links among the instruments in particular markets are increasingly close, as the seemingly different markets become integrated (e.g., the deposit and credit, insurance and capital markets), the economy evolves in connection with the Information Communication Technologies (ICT), and the knowledge-based economy and financialisation develop.

In the conditions of a perfectly competitive, complete market described in the Arrow-Debreu-McKenzie (ADM) model, there is no place for financial intermediation (cf. Allen and Gale, 2001, pp. 127–149; Arrow, 1951, 1964; Debreu, 1959; Panek, 2003, pp. 147–163). In the model of perfect capital market based on the ADM model, the following assumptions are made:

- a No market participant has impact on prices.
- b The terms and conditions of lending and borrowing are identical for all market participants and constant.
- c There are no taxes.
- d There are no economies of scale.
- e All financial instruments are homogeneous, divisible and convertible.
- f There are no costs of information, transactions or insolvency.
- g All market participants have ex ante and ex post prompt and full information about factors and developments related to the future values of financial instruments in trade.

In these conditions of a full symmetry of information and the absence of market risk or any transactional costs, transactions take place directly between market participants. The model is undoubtedly a valuable teaching aid and a system of reference for the analysis of processes in the real world of finance. We can only state how far "the real world" is from the model assumptions.

The imperfection of financial markets is the cause of financial intermediation. This imperfection comprises risk and uncertainty, transaction costs, the asymmetry of information, taxes, diverse financial conditions of market participants and their access to loans, varied financial products and externalities. Financial intermediation at least partly overcomes these imperfections. In theory, each is assigned a different weight as a reason for development of financial intermediation.

In the traditional theory of financial intermediation, financial institutions (banks and insurance companies) are intermediaries between savers and investors. They collect savings and convert them into capital to effectively allocate the capital to the economy in the conditions of information asymmetry and risk. Diamond and Dybvig (1983) treat banks as coalitions of deposit holders expected to provide households with "insurance" against idiosyncratic shocks[1] that may affect their liquidity. The literature also emphasises that financial intermediaries have knowledge based on integrated information about the operation of the economy and financial market, which helps them invest their customers' capitals effectively (cf. Leland and Pyle, 1977).

Merton and Bodie (Merton, 1993; Merton and Bodie, 1995) suggest that the financial system should be analysed from a functional, institutional perspective. The institutional approach was prevalent to begin with, that is, an analysis of the financial system as a system of institutions intermediary between those who supply and those who need capital. The functional approach involves an analysis of the financial system from the viewpoint of the services provided and value added to the customer. Financial institutions launch new types of assets (financial instruments) competing for customers. The nature and functions of financial intermediation and the structure of the financial product range are influenced by macroeconomic and technological transformations in the economy. This is especially evident in connection with the emergence of the so-called knowledge-based or new economy. Interestingly, this approach refers back to J. Schumpeter's theory of entrepreneur and innovation (1960) and highlights the unique functions of financial intermediation that are important to economic growth and development and consist in the mobilisation of savings, allocation of capital, risk management, transaction facilitation and business monitoring. In view of Schumpeter's theory, it can be said that the process of "creative destruction" also takes place in the case of financial institutions and intermediation, resulting in financial development, a component of economic development.

The revolution in information and ICT technologies has had a major impact on transforming the functions of financial intermediation and changing the relations between financial intermediation institutions and financial instrument market and has accelerated the emergence of financial innovations.

First, the scale of information asymmetry and costs of transactions have diminished. The time of closing financial transactions is reduced. The narrower asymmetry of information has allowed for more transactions between saving holders and investors without intermediation in the open market.

Financial assets have been commoditised since the use of new ICT methods in transactions requires uniform financial products. In parallel, tailor-made products and services have started playing an increasing role in addressing specific conditions and customer needs. This is known as the so-called customising of financial product, the effect of adapting a financial product to customer requirements (cf. Scholtens and van Wensveen, 2003).

The asymmetry of information reduced by a more common access to macro- and microeconomic and financial information does not mean, however, that financial institutions have fallen victim to the ICT revolution. On the contrary, they are its beneficiaries. Their role in alleviating the asymmetry of information is smaller at the expense of their growing role in providing the financial market players with unique information as an integral part of their financial intermediation function.

Financial intermediation institutions, by developing financial innovations, create new needs for ICT products, thus stimulating continued technological progress (see Scholtens and van Wensveen, 2003).

The development of e-banking and e-finance is certainly an example. Information innovations have an increasing impact on the development of financial products and risk management.

Financial innovation increasingly relates to the management of currency risk, interest rate risk and credit risk.

B. Scholtens and D. van Wensveen (2003) point to an important characteristic of financial intermediation, namely, the creation of added value incorporated in financial instruments for savers and investors. These types of instruments cannot be created jointly or individually by savers and investors. That process of value creation is intensified by a competition among the existing financial institutions and those that enter the market and launch financial innovations. Financial institutions must continue analysing the preferences of the financial market participants and translate these preferences into features of new financial products. Risk transformation is an essential function of financial intermediation institutions. By creating financial instruments absorbing risks, they create the added value. This way, the sector of financial intermediation institutions has turned into a sector of financial industry (cf. also Allen and Santomero, 1997; Merton and Bodie, 1995; Allen and Gale, 2001).

It has been mentioned before that the relationship between the role and place of the financial intermediation institutions (banks, insurance companies, investment funds, etc.) in the market and financial instrument markets has changed, too. In the traditional system, households of lower savings and assets and small- and medium-sized enterprises were the direct customers of financial intermediaries, supplying savings and borrowing (see Allen and Gale, 2001, pp. 471–472).

As part of the state-of-the-art system resulting from the above developments connected with the knowledge-based economy, households and small- and medium-sized enterprises are the clients of financial intermediation institutions that help invest the monies from their clients in the market of financial instruments (especially those quoted at organised exchanges) and offer products based on quoted financial instruments. Large firms, in turn, mostly take advantage of monies obtained directly from the organised capital markets (exchanges). This is a result of the factors described above, which have caused financial intermediation institutions to become the providers of financial services creating added values. This state of affairs also indicates a rising role of financial markets in the economy, which may have even become "the heart" of the financial system and the market economy, "pumping" money and information in various forms (see Allen and Gale, 2001, pp. 471–472).

General institutional and regulatory characteristics

The first breakthrough programme for the development of a single internal market in the European Union (EU) was the A. Cockfield White Paper. The report defined barriers to the establishment and operation of the single internal market and proposed 282 draft legal acts expected to overcome the existing barriers. The programme was accepted by the member states. Its key objective was to realise five fundamental freedoms of commodity, goods, person, service and capital flows. The goal was the removal of the market and trade barriers existing in the already competitive markets, the opening of new markets and sectors of the economy to competition, the convergence of laws prevailing in the particular countries of the community that directly affect the single market and the realisation of community policies supporting the creation and efficient operation of the single market. The programme abandoned the idea of a full harmonisation of markets in the individual countries for the sake of the principle of a mutual recognition of the rules prevailing in the particular member states. The realisation of the White Paper's assumptions was fostered with the adoption of the Single European Act in 1987 and then of the European Union Treaty in Maastricht in 1992. The approval of the Lisbon Strategy in 2000 was the next stage of providing the conditions for a single financial market. The Strategy emphasised that the development of an effective, integrated financial market in the EU is important to the development of the knowledge-based economy as such a market should play a key role in supporting the development and use of new technologies and thus the creation of new jobs. It should be noted that the Strategy's assumptions and objectives have never been fully put into practice.

The formation of the Economic and Monetary Union on 1 January 1999 and the introduction of the single currency was a major breakthrough in the financial markets' integration in the EU. The introduction of Euro substantially accelerated the integration of financial markets in the EU. First of all, a single currency involves the elimination of the currency exchange risk in 17 countries of the EU. This provided for a large financial market of a high liquidity.

The influence of Euro on the financial markets' integration in the EU cannot be isolated from other factors like globalisation, advanced technologies or the reforms of financial market regulations. These facts suggest that the Euro has had a unique effect on the homogenisation of financial markets and the introduction of new products and techniques starting from 1999 (cf. EC, 2004, pp. 119–130).

The single financial market in the EU is part and parcel of the single internal market. The operation of the single financial market and of the entire single market in the EU is based on the free flow of capitals and payments, the freedom of establishment and service provision. The principle of the so-called single licence is the basic factor determining the process of integration of the EU member states' financial markets. This means that a financial institution (including banks, insurance companies and investment fund societies) can provide its services in other member states by force of a financial activity licence (permit) obtained in its mother country without the need to have special licences issued elsewhere. However, its activities outside the native country are subject to the jurisdiction of a host country.

The adoption of this rule required the institution in the EU of minimum requirements of financial institutions that prevail in all the member states. They apply, among other things, to capital equipment, the so-called prudential rules. "The principle of the native state's supervision and of mutual recognition" is another crucial rule. Accordingly, firms operating legally in a given country can function in another EU member state subject to the same conditions as in their native country – based on the mutual recognition of their standards (cf. Nieborak, 2008, pp. 99–101).

The harmonisation of law concerning the operation of particular markets is a major factor determining the process of financial markets' integration in the EU. The Financial Services Action Plan (FSAP) is a step in this direction. It was approved by the European Commission in May 1999 following on a consultation of *Financial Services. Building a Framework for Action* published in 1998. The FSAP was not a plan of a single financial market, but a mostly legal definition of the project that opened the path for the emergence of such a market (see Janicka, 2005, p. 42).

It was the FSAP's overarching objective to improve the conditions for efficient functioning of the single financial market. Five goals are specified as part of this objective:

a The possibility of obtaining financing on good terms across the EU.
b The free access of investors to all the EU markets.
c Allowing financial providers for an unrestricted provision of services across the EU.
d Allowing management entities to allocate assets to the most productive undertakings.
e Providing market players with conditions for free transactions that aren't exposed to the risk of settlement systems.

The FSAP encompassed three additional strategic objectives, including appropriate goals. The first strategic objective – "creation of a single wholesale market of financial services" – comprised 19 goals making up six groupings:

a Obtaining capital in the European dimension.
b A shared legal framework for an integrated market of securities and derivatives.
c Single standards of financial reporting for quoted companies.
d Limiting the systemic risk in transaction accounting.
e Safe and transparent conditions of transborder transactions.
f A single market for investors.

The attainment of these goals was expected to provide issuers with the competitive conditions of obtaining capital, to provide investors and issuers with a free market access, the possibility of offering transborder services freely, establishment of a transparent and integrated supervisory structure, and to guarantee a secure execution and settlement of financial transactions.

The second strategic objective – "the creation of an open and secure retail market for financial services" – encompassed nine goals intended inter alia to clearly define the rights of financial institution customers and assure their access to information, to remove differences between national regulations of transactions with retail customers, to create new distribution channels of financial services on a European scale and to form safe and effective systems of accounting for transborder retail transactions.

The third strategic objective – "the preparation of supervisory regulations and a financial supervision system" – comprised ten goals, with the elimination of gaps in the prevailing prudential standards, development of the banking sector standards in the EU and creation of EU-level integrated supervisory structures as the most important.[2] The FSAP was to be implemented by April 2004. Thirty directives putting the FSAP's goals and objective into effect had been prepared by that date. Beginning in 2005, the stage of transfer of the directive provisions and enforcement of their application in the EU member states commenced.

The establishment of a comprehensive package of financial market regulations and levelling differences between the legal systems in the individual EU member states in this area was an undoubted achievement of the FSAP (cf. Pilecka, 2009, p. 41).

The so-called Green Paper was published in May 2005, containing a set of the European Commission proposals for continuing the actions initiated as part of the FSAP. New legislative initiatives were to be taken in exceptional circumstances, whereas action should focus on a simplification and standardisation of the existing range of financial services regulations. The existing regulation of the financial market was found too complicated, therefore.

The so-called White Paper was published on 5 December 2005, which advanced a strategy of action on financial services in 2005–2010. It envisaged five strategic objectives:

a An enhanced integration of the financial market.
b The application of the "better lawmaking" principle.
c The construction of proper supervisory structures.
d Enhanced competitiveness among entities offering financial services, in particular, in the retail services markets.
e A strengthening of the EU's status in the globalising financial markets by setting global standards, the development of cooperation in this area with the United States and other countries, and through a strong representation of the EU in international organisations (cf. Pilecka, 2009, pp. 35–37).

In 2000, the EU's Economic and Financial Affairs Council (ECOFIN) decided to appoint a seven-member Committee of Wise Man on Securities

Markets Regulation headed by A. Lamfalussy. It was tasked with compiling a report on the operation of securities market in the EU and with formulating recommendations for necessary reforms. The final version of the so-called Lamfalussy's Report was submitted in February 2001. Its key conclusion said that the financial market regulations were too complicated, inflexible and improperly introduced. The Report recommended a new way of lawmaking and formation of European committees responsible for the financial market regulations. The process of lawmaking should consist of four levels (see Nieborak, 2008, pp. 88–91):

Level I – framework directives adopted by the European Parliament and the Council comprise general regulations and those determining the extent of authorisations to issue detailed provisions.

Level II – the issue of detailed regulations following on consultations; these regulations are developed as part of cooperation between the EU member states, the European Commission and two auxiliary committees (e.g., the European Securities Committee, European Banking Committee or the European Employee Insurance and Pensions Committee).

Level III – including the basic means to the implementation of the decisions made at levels I and II, with an important role played by the authorities grouping the regulators of the particular EU member states (the Committee of European Securities Supervisors, the Committee of European Banking Supervisors, the Committee of European Insurance and Pension Supervisors).

Level IV – the European Commission supervises the application of the adopted legal regulations.

On 5 November 2003, the European Commission presented a draft directive establishing a new regulatory and organisational structure for the financial market as recommended by Lamfalussy's Report. The directive was approved by the Parliament and the Council (the Directive of the European Parliament and Council No. 2005/1/EC of 9 March 2005, OJL No. 79 of 24 March 2005). The European Commission proceeded to issue some decisions establishing the following authorities: the European Banking Committee, the European Employee Insurance and Pension Committee, the European Committee of Banking Supervisors and the European Committee of Insurance and Premium Supervision.

The implementation of Lamfalussy's process improved the legislative process in respect of the regulation and integration of financial markets. This contributed to a relatively efficient implementation of the FSAP.

The harmonisation of law, namely, a minimum single regulation for all countries that would assure the security of economic trade, plays a major role in the process of financial market integration. The Basel Capital Accord is the foundation in the banking sector.

The Basel Committee on Banking Supervision passed the so-called Basel Capital Accord (Basel I) in 1988. It introduced some risk-weighted capital requirements for both balance and off-balance items. It was the first all-round international treaty concerning capital requirements, which set equal conditions for banks active in the international market.

In June 2004, the Basel Committee on Banking Supervision published the final version of the New Capital Accord (Basel II), intended to boost the security and stability of the international banking system, to improve the methods of setting bank capital requirements depending on the level of risk and scale of operations, and to take a fuller account of recent financial innovations when determining capital adequacy.

Basel II's provisions have become the law prevailing in all the EU states by means of the European Parliament's and the Council's directives,[3] jointly referred to as the Capital Requirements Directive (CRD).

The New Capital Accord consists of three supplementary pillars:

- *Pillar I* – concerning the estimation of minimum capital requirements relating to the credit, market and operational risks. Like in the 1988 Accord and its 1996 amendment, the minimum capital requirements rest on three basic elements: the definition of regulatory capital, risk-weighted assets and a minimum relation of capital to risk-weighted assets, formulated as follows:

$$R = \left[FW/AWR + 12.5 \times (WKRR + WKRO)\right] \times 100\% \tag{1.1}$$

  where:
  R – the solvency ratio,
  FW – equity,
  AWR – total risk-weighted off-balance assets and liabilities computed for the credit risk,
  WKRR – capital requirements due to the market risk,
  WKRO – capital requirements due to the operating risk.

  The overall solvency ratio cannot be lower than 8%. The regulatory capital (equity) is divided into three categories: initial capital (Tier 1), supplementary capital (Tier 2) and the third category capital (Tier 3).
- *Pillar II* – it defines encouraging banks to apply internal models for the estimation of capital requirements and setting of target capitals in accordance with a given bank's risk profile and internal risk control techniques as the basic role of banking supervision.
- *Pillar III* – it obliges banks to maintain an appropriate market discipline and authorises them to disclose information on their risk profile and levels of capitalisation.

Some regulations of financial conglomerates were introduced as well.[4] A definition of financial conglomerates was offered and single rules of their financial supervision were set. The institution of additional supervision for financial conglomerates was introduced, a supervision coordinator, selected depending on the status and significance of regulated entities in a conglomerate's structure, and their duties were defined.[5]

The Markets in Financial Instruments Directive (MiFID) plays an important regulatory role with reference to the capital market.[6] It was issued in order to:

a Ensure a proper management and settlement of any systemic risks in transborder accounts and settlements.
b Promote the integration of accounts and settlements pushed by the market forces by removing interferences with competition.
c Assure proper transparency and supervisory solutions.

The primary purpose of the directive is to enhance competition in the investment services market, improve the transparency of investment operations and customer support processes and assure conformity of transactions with orders placed by customers. The MiFID governs and allows investment firms to provide their services to investors across the EU without the need to meet additional requirements set by national laws. It also enables the EU citizens to take advantage of investment services according to standard rules and to cut the costs of transborder accounts and settlements.

The trade in instruments out of the public markets was regulated as well, which offered some new opportunities for the development of the market as a whole. Customer protection is the crucial objective of the directive. Investment enterprises are bound to act fairly, honestly and professionally in the best interests of customers. Information addressed by an investment enterprise to its customers should be reliable, indubitable and not misleading. Moreover, information on financial instruments and proposed investment strategies should include appropriate guidelines and warnings of risks inherent in investing in such instruments.

Added to all that, single minimum requirements of the prospectus and transparency of information about the capital market players are set.[7] Community-wide regulations of confidential information and risk handling are very important for safe trade in the single financial market.[8]

The Community-wide regulation was applied to investment funds and enterprises managing the funds, too.[9] The "single European passport" was introduced, which means that the enterprises managing (group) investment funds can operate all across the EU by force of permits secured under the laws of their native EU member states. The pan-European validity of such a permit means the possibility of providing services and of establishment by forming a branch in another country, among other actions. The regulation also covered the rules of supervision over enterprises managing investment funds.

The introduction of the International Accounting Standards to the EU countries was a major factor affecting the integration of financial markets.[10] The standardisation of accounting, including financial reporting, is a great improvement for enterprises, investors, investment firm clients and members of investment funds, introducing the transparency of financial information, single rules for reporting requirements of quoted companies and books of accounts.

The creation of a single system of settlements and payments on the EU's scale is fundamental to the process of financial market integration.

The TARGET (Trans European Automated Real Time Gross Settlement Express Transfer) settlement system was created by combining decentralised national systems of Euro real time gross settlements (RTGS) and the payment mechanism of the European Central Bank. It was launched in January 1999. In time, the EU countries from outside the Euro area joined the system. To prepare for an expansion of the Euro area, the Eurosystem developed a second generation of TARGET, or TARGET2, pursuant to a decision of the ECB Governing Council dated 2002. The TARGET2 was put into effect in the second half of 2007. The shared technical platform was started on 19 November 2007.[11]

A strengthening of the EU as a financial centre was an intention of the TARGET2, to be assured by the system's neutrality, exhibited in its following characteristics:

a The banking systems of the country members of the TARGET2 will be treated equally, with no preferential status. The system will be politically, geographically and economically neutral.
b Central and commercial banks will have the same rights to the services provided by the TARGET2.
c All the participants will pay the same rates of fees.
d The operating principles of the TARGET2 will comply with the decentralised structure of the Eurosystem.

The TARGET2 system brings the following novelties (compared to its older version):

a A standardisation of the scope and level of services available to the participants from all the member countries.
b A single fee structure in the entire system.
c A technical consolidation of the system.
d Faster transfer (fewer delays, as there are fewer conversions between different systems).
e A simplified scheme of payments.
f A modular design of core and optional modules.
g Enhanced resistance to breakdowns.

The TARGET2 is among the top payment systems worldwide, beside the American FEDWIRE, and the CLS system for currency settlements on a global scale. The TARGET2 is also referred to as "the systems' system" since it will be used by more than 60 other payment and similar systems.

The SEPA (Single Euro Payments Area) project, developed by the European Payments Council (EPC), set up by the European banking community and actively supported by the European Commission, the European Parliament and the European Central Bank, is another step towards the improvement of settlement and payment systems.

The SEPA is designed to introduce mechanisms for effective Euro payments in Europe and to treat this area as a local market, with all the consequences associated with the time of transaction execution and fees (i.e., the equalisation of these parameters for domestic and transborder Euro payments). The project was put into practice in 2010 and the process of transferring settlements there is currently in progress.

This is an outline of key institutional solutions and regulations affecting the process of financial market integration in the EU, including the Euro area. In spite of their frequently excessive detail and great complication, they have played a major role in removing barriers to the integration processes by harmonising institutional, including legal, foundations of financial markets and the entire financial sector in the EU. This doesn't mean, though, that the present system of regulations suffers from no defects, as it is first of all inconsistent and overly complicated (see, Larosiere, 2009). This is due to the evolutionary process of EU lawmaking in this respect and commonly to a tendency towards over-regulation of phenomena in financial markets. This is typical for any bureaucracy that begins a life of its own at a certain point. This has long been the case of the EU bureaucracy. This is probably inevitable. Any initiatives of any regulations, in particular of the EU financial markets, should be followed carefully. The regulation is certainly in order; yet, certain important aspects should be borne in mind:

- a An appropriate balance between financial supervision, prudential rules and economic freedom.
- b The creation of the rules of the game, not detailed regulation of individual conduct (the latter is never successful or effective, while any bureaucracy suffers from this tendency).
- c The minimisation of transaction costs.
- d Ensuring transparency of the financial market and market play.
- e Openness to financial innovation and a system of the rules of the game to secure the interests of all market players.
- f The prevention of excessive interdependences among financial institutions.
- g Care for financial institutions that are safe and innovative for customers.
- h An improved market discipline and a system of early warning signals of a crisis.

The European Commission adopted a document and work thus began to reform the principles of financial market regulation and creation of a new financial supervision architecture in the EU.[12]

The formation of the European Systemic Risk Board (ESRB) and of three European Supervisory Authorities (ESA) to replace the earlier European supervisor committees (CEBS, CEIOPS, CESR), known as the third level of Lamfalussy's procedure committees, was a key part of the financial supervision reform in the EU. The newly founded authorities are based in the same locations as their respective Committees, namely, London, Frankfurt and Paris. The new financial supervision system in the EU has been in place since 1 January 2011 (cf. www.knf.gov.pl).

The main purpose of this system is to assure a proper implementation of the regulations concerning the financial sector so as to preserve financial stability and ensure confidence in the financial system as a whole and an adequate protection of financial service consumers.

The European System of Financial Supervision consists of:

a European Systemic Risk Board – ESRB.
b European Supervisory Authorities – ESA.
c European Banking Authority – EBA.
d European Insurance and Occupational Pensions Authority – EIOPA.
e European Securities and Markets Authority – ESMA.
f Joint Committee of European Supervisory Authorities.
g Competent authorities or supervisory authorities of the member states specified in the appropriate EU laws.

The Basel Committee on Banking Supervision also formulated a New Capital Accord, Basel III. The following assumptions underlie the changes:

a Enhance banks' capacity for absorbing external shocks and reduce the risk of shock transmission to the real economy.
b A more restrictive approach to capital requirements – a narrower regulatory capital and a universal requirement of a bank's financial leverage.
c A mechanism of anti-cyclical policy of dynamic reserve and write-off creation and capital buffering at times of strong credit expansion.

The capital bank regulations prevailing in the EU are based on the CRD IV/CRR package: Directive 2013/36/EU (CRD), to be implemented in domestic laws, and Regulation 575/2013 (Capital Requirements Regulation, CRR), directly applicable to all the member states of the EU. These regulations rely on the Basel Committee on Banking Supervision guidelines, the so-called Basel III (BCBS, 2011, 2013).

The new solutions primarily relate to:

a The improvement of the quality and transparency of banks' capital base – to assure that the banking system is better capable of absorbing losses (both in operation and after it discontinues).
b The extension of the scope of risks included in the capital standard – added to the earlier solutions concerning the commercial portfolio and securitisation transactions (Basel 2.5), new capital requirements are formulated for the contractor's credit risk arising from derivative transactions, repo transactions and the financing of securities.
c The introduction of standards promoting capital buffers and a more prospective approach to the creation of provisions (the model of provisions against expected but not incurred losses) – to limit the existing procyclicality of the regulations and the impact of shocks (instead of intensifying them like at present), resulting in an improved stability of the banking sector and its lower liability to external shocks.
d The introduction of a financial leverage ratio as a supplement to the solvency ratio – to prevent excessive leveraging of financial institutions (an excessive growth of the financial leverage levels) and to provide additional security against the risk model and measurement errors.
e The introduction of minimum liquidity standards and measures to facilitate the monitoring and assessment of the risk of liquidity loss.

The stricter definition of basic (Tier 1) and supplementary (Tier 2) equities, a definition of a more rigorous category of common equity tier 1 (CET1), a longer list of equity reductions that can be referred to CET1 and resignation from the option of meeting solvency ratio requirements using short-term (Tier 3) capital deserve particular attention in the first group of modifications.

Besides defining the requirement of minimum solvency ratio (total and for CET1), capital buffers are introduced:

a Capital conservation buffer – 2.5% of the total risk exposure.
b An anti-cyclical buffer specific to an institution – set by a competent authority, it must be in the range of 0–2.5% (the maximum level can be exceeded, e.g., for reasons of a cyclical systemic risk or guidelines of the ESRB).
c Global systemically important institutions (G-SIIs) buffer – depending on an institution's subcategory (1–3.5%).
d Other systemically important institutions (O-SIIs) buffer – up to 2%.
e Systemic risk buffer – it may apply to an entire financial sector or at least one of its subsets in a member state. It's set as 1–5% of the exposures present in a given state.

The standard solvency ratio is supplemented with a simple ratio of financial leverage, a relation of basic equity (Tier 1 capital) to total exposure (the total value of exposure arising from all assets and off-balance items that are not deducted when computing the Tier 1 capital). A required level (or levels) of this ratio will be determined after a period of observation starting in 2018. The preliminary assumption is that banks would be required to maintain this measure at a minimum of 3%.

The experience of the most recent financial crisis demonstrated the significance of management of banks' liquidity risk. As a consequence of gaps in this area, new short-term (LCR) and long-term (NSFR) liquidity standards have been imposed on banks.

The introduction of the Liquidity Coverage Ratio (LCR)[13] is to promote the short-term resistance of banks to the liquidity risk by making sure that they have sufficient high-liquidity resources to survive extraordinary occurrences in the financial market that continue for more than a month.

The Net Stable Funding Ratio (NSFR)[14] has a year's horizon and serves a more balanced maturity structure of assets, equity and liabilities in a bank.

Regulations concerning the insurance sector and markets

The single insurance market is part of the integrated financial market in the EU, in turn, part of the single internal market for goods, commodities, capital and labour, in place since 1993. Unlike other sectors, the insurance market, like banking, is still highly regulated despite the ongoing process of deregulation. This is largely due to the unique nature of insurance companies, treated as public trust organisations, since they hold funds entrusted by policyholders. The regulations of insurance market relate in particular to the solvency of insurance companies and are expressions of care for the interests of insurance contract beneficiaries.

According to L. Oręziak (1996), the formation of the single insurance market, like in the case of other financial market segments, is an attempt at ensuring an adequate market competition that enforces both an improved quality of its services and a reduction of their prices. The need to face the growing competition from the US and Japanese financial institutions was an important motivation. The changes in place and in progress are ultimately to serve consumers, that is, the clients of insurance services. They are individuals, institutions and enterprises. In particular, the possibility of securing insurance protection at lower costs is not without an impact on enterprise effectiveness and thus competitive standing against American and Japanese firms.

The single insurance market in the EU was formed gradually as set out in the Rome (1957) and Maastricht (1992) Treaties, namely:

- The freedom of establishment – governed by Articles 52–56 of the Rome Treaty. It assumes that private individuals and corporate entities have the right to run free business activities in all the EU member states. Accordingly, financial institutions, including insurance companies, can found branches or offices.

- The freedom of service provision – governed by Articles 59–66 of the Rome Treaty. Accordingly, an entity based in a member state can provide its services to entities from other EU countries where it has no branches or local offices. Thus, transborder services can be offered without taking advantage of the freedom of establishment.
- The freedom of capital flow – regulated by Article 73b of Maastricht Treaty, which prohibits restrictions to capital flows among the EU countries and between the EU and third-party countries. The Treaty also regulated the EU members' actions as part of the domestic supervision of financial institutions and their obedience to tax legislation (see Monkiewicz and Monkiewicz, 2005, p. 49).

The process of building the single insurance market in the EU was initiated as long back as the 1970s. The directives issued in 1973 (regarding non-life insurance) and 1979 (life insurance) specified the conditions for insurance companies exercising the basic Rome Treaty freedom, namely, the so-called freedom of establishment. It denotes the right to undertake independent economic activities in other EU member states under the legislation of these countries relating to their own citizens. The other freedom essential to the single market, i.e., the freedom of services, was to be supported with the so-called Second Directive (22 June 1988 and 8 November 1990). The process of constructing an integrated insurance market culminated in the so-called Third Generation Directives (18 June 1992 and 10 November 1992). They introduced the principle of issuing the so-called single insurance licence. If an insurance institution secures such a licence in one EU country, it can provide its services in the remaining EU member states without obtaining separate permits there. It can set up branches in those countries or provide its services from its registered address (across frontiers). Like in respect of banks, an insurance institution is supervised by its native country. To prevent insurers from basing their operations in a country of minimum requirements, joint minimum requirements of all the institutions of this type have been set across the EU in order to protect the interests of their customers. Insurance institutions, like banks, are treated as public trust institutions, while their efficient operation affects the security of an entire financial system of a state.

The assurance of free capital flows within the EU became important to the operation of a single insurance market. The very process of liberalisation of capital movements turned out to be long-lasting and rather complicated. From the perspective of the insurance market, the free capital flow in the EU means that every entity based or residing in a member state may freely transfer premiums to other member states. Insurance companies, however, are free to make payments of compensations and benefits. From the insurers' viewpoint, the possibility of financial investments all across the EU is an extraordinarily important effect of the capital flow liberalisation. Insurance companies are among major institutional investors in the financial market.

The possibility of finding safe and profitable investments is crucial to their effective operation and profitability. The existence of a global financial market where capitals can move freely enables insurance companies to make optimum choices considering various aspects of their activities.

Ensuring the liquidity of insurance companies is a major aspect of the single insurance market regulation. The solvency is intended to protect the interests of policyholders and the insured and, to some extent, constitutes the point of insurance. Signing a contract with an insolvent insurer doesn't provide for insurance cover and the insurance fails to discharge its basic functions that express its essence and sense. It's for this reason that solvency issues are regulated by law in prudential standards that should be followed by insurance companies in the insurance market. At its simplest, the solvency of an insurance company can be defined as a long-term ability to meet all of its liabilities on time. This is not the sole definition. Specialist literature offers a variety of takes on the concept, as reviewed in Table 1.1.

These notions of solvency stress the need to secure an insurance company's liabilities arising from the contracts of insurance. This is achieved with:

- A proper (adequate) value of assets in excess of liabilities.
- Appropriate cash flows that allow to repay liabilities, securing financial liquidity.

Such a concept of solvency encompasses both the static and dynamic (cash) aspects, though it must be pointed out that they do not always arise jointly. Some authors focus on the former only (e.g., Müllers Report), others only on the latter (Kastelijn and Remmerswaal, 1986; Coutts and Devit, 1989). Obviously, there are some definitions combining the two aspects (Sandstrom, 2006; Bijak, 2009; Hardie *et al.*, 1986). It seems that the concept should comprise both these aspects as the realisation of only one in fact fails to assure the solvency: holding assets that can't be used to meet liabilities, as it would involve their substantial freezing, for instance, or a reverse situation, where the assets of an appropriate financial liquidity that can be used to repay liabilities are not even up to the level of liabilities. Thus, an insurance company that at the same time handles the static (holds assets at least up to its liabilities) and dynamic (holds real cash flows above its liabilities) aspects is solvent. An adequate risk management in an insurance company needs to be highlighted as well, since without it, appropriate assets to secure liabilities or their appropriate quality to guarantee the realisation of current cash flows would be impossible.

Based on these concepts of an insurance company's solvency, the causes of its insolvency can be determined. They are listed in Table 1.2.

The assessment of insurance companies' solvency is regulated by Directive 2009/138/EC (*Solvency II*). Besides the basic directive, some second-level regulations include delegated and executive acts in the form of the European Commission regulations and third-level regulations include

Table 1.1 Selected concepts of insurance company solvency

Author(s)	*Year*	*Concept of solvency*
J. Łazowski	1934	Financial security of an insurance company.
L. Pokorzyński	1957	Realisation of the principle of reality of insurance protection.
W.M. Kastelijn, J.C.M. Remmerswaal	1986	Financial resources sufficient to meet all monetary liabilities.
Faculty of Actuaries – Hardie *et al.*	1986	Meeting current or any future liabilities subject to possible assumptions and to a specific degree of likelihood.
T. Pentikainen	1989	The notion of solvency is only referred to state supervision: the protection of interests of the insured and beneficiaries under contracts of insurance and the need for a supervisor's prompt action in case of threats.
Y. Kahane	1989	A function of all aspects of an insurance company depends on a great number of parameters connected with its operation, including external factors.
S. Coutts, R. Devit	1989	The situation where revenue from assets is adequate to the meeting of required spending on liabilities (based on the definition of an insurance company's insolvency).
H. Rubin	1995	Minimum requirements of an insurance company's healthy financial situation, where assets are larger than liabilities.
S. Conant, N.L. Desoutler, D.L. Long, R. Macgrogan	1996	• Current solvency – the condition of an insurance company's positive net value. It corresponds to a situation where the total value of assets is greater than that of liabilities, that is, the capitalisation is adequate, or where the difference between the current value of expected flows from assets held by the insurance company and the current value of expected flows from existing liabilities discounted at a set rate of interest is positive. • Technical solvency – an insurance company's ability to meet its current liabilities. This means that cash and current assets must exceed the required liabilities in a valuation at arm's length.
Müllers Report	1997	A proper volume of an insurance company's financial resources, in fact, the difference between the assets and liabilities of an insurance company.
J.F. Outreville	1998	A situation where assets are greater than payable compensations.
International Association of Insurance Supervisors (IAIS)	2000	An insurance company's ability to meet its liabilities under all contracts at any time.
W. Bijak	2003	The value of assets free from any liabilities to the insured, defined as the security buffer.
A. Sandstrom	2006	Security for the duration of all contracts of insurance in place.

(*Continued*)

Table 1.1 Selected concepts of insurance company solvency (*Continued*)

Author(s)	*Year*	*Concept of solvency*
W. Bijak	2009	A dynamic equilibrium between an insurance company's assets, liabilities under contracts of insurance in place and cash flows generated by the assets and liabilities. Such a state is very likely to guarantee that an insurance company will meet its liabilities to the insured, policyholders or beneficiaries under contracts of insurance in variable natural, economic and social conditions. This is a situation where internal resources, structures and processes of an insurer and external structures where it is situated have no systemic effect on a diminishing likelihood of the insurer meeting its liabilities.
M. Lament	2013	An insurance company is solvent if it handles its static aspect, holding assets at least to the level of liabilities, and dynamic aspect, holding real cash flows in excess of liabilities, at the same time.
J.W. Euphasio, J.V.F. Carvalho	2020	An insurance company's ability to meet its liabilities in case of a grave adverse operational shock.

Source: The authors' own research on the basis of Łazowski (1934), Pokorzyński (1957), Kastelijn and Remmerswaal (1986), Hardie *et al.* (1986), Pantikainen *et al.* (1989), Kahane *et al.* (1989), Coutts and Devit (1989), Rubin (1995), Conant *et al.* (1996), Müllers Report (1997), Outreville (1998), IAIS (2000), Bijak (2003, 2009), Sandstrom (2006), Lament (2013) and Euphasio and Carvalho (2020).

binding technical standards and non-binding guidelines and recommendations of EIOPA apply as well.

An extensive codification and reform of the framework of insurance activities in the EU, as well as an EU-wide harmonisation related to a solvency assessment system of insurance and reinsurance companies, including their financial economics and the supervision process, are the subject matter of *Solvency II*.

In line with Article 1 of *Solvency II*, the scope of regulation comprises the following issues:

- The undertaking and conduct of direct insurance and reinsurance on own account in the Community.
- Supervision of insurance and reinsurance groups.
- Reorganisation and liquidation of insurance companies.

The directive prevails in the EU countries: Norway, Liechtenstein and Iceland. It applies to direct life and non-life and reinsurance companies where:

1 The written premium is above €5 m a year.
2 Total gross technical provisions of an insurance company are in excess of €25 m, including the shares of reinsurers and special purpose vehicles.[15]

Table 1.2 The causes of insurance companies' insolvency – According to selected authors

Author(s)	*Year*	*Causes of insolvency*
J. Łazowski	1934	Lack of appropriate supervision of insurance companies, ineffective insurance supervision.
L. Pokorzyński	1957	Lack of financial or material coverage of compensations payable.
W.M. Kastelijn, J.C.M. Remmerswaal	1986	Lack of funds to cover liabilities.
Faculty of Actuaries – Hardie *et al.*	1986	Lack of financial liquidity; assets are insufficient to cover liabilities.
T. Pentikainen	1989	Improper management of insurance risk that leads to the introduction of appropriate prudential regulations and public supervision. All economic actions and decision-making processes of the insurance company influence solvency.
Y. Kahane	1989	All the aspects of operations.
S. Coutts, R. Devit	1989	Revenue is inadequate to spending on liabilities.
H. Rubin	1995	Liabilities exceed assets. A poor financial position of the insurance company.
S. Conant, N.L. Desoutler, D.L. Long, R. Macgrogan	1996	• Current solvency – too high liabilities, inadequate capitalisation. • Technical solvency – improper Asset Liability Management (ALM).
Müllers Report	1997	Assets are inadequate to liabilities.
J.F. Outreville	1998	Excessive compensation liabilities.
International Association of Insurance Supervisors *(IAIS)*	2000	Assets are not enough to meet claims (liabilities), lack of financial liquidity.
W. Bijak	2003	Lack of assets free from any liabilities.
A. Sandstrom	2006	Lack of funds to pay compensations and benefits.
W. Bijak	2009	Failure to meet liabilities due to a low value of assets or of cash flows, or due to the impact of internal or external structures.
J. Lisowski	2010	Poor financial standing, unwillingness to meet liabilities, no legal guarantees of insurance protection.
M. Lament	2013	Inappropriate value of assets relative to liabilities. Lack of real cash flows.
J.W. Euphasio, J.V.F. Carvalho	2020	Improper reinsurance treaties.

Source: The authors' own research on the basis of Łazowski (1934), Pokorzyński (1957), Kastelijn and Remmerswaal (1986), Hardie *et al.* (1986), Pantikainen *et al.* (1989), Kahane *et al.* (1989), Coutts and Devit (1989), Rubin (1995), Conant *et al.* (1996), Müllers Report (1997), Outreville (1998), IAIS (2000), Bijak (2003, 2009), Sandstrom (2006), Lisowski (2010), Lament (2013) and Euphasio and Carvalho (2020).

3 The inward reinsurance activities of a company are in excess of:

a €0.5 m of gross written premium.
b €2.5 m of gross technical provisions, including the shares of reinsurers and special purpose vehicles.
c The gross written premium of an inward reinsurance company is above 10% of gross written premium.
d The gross written premium of an inward reinsurance company is above 10% of gross technical provisions, including the shares of reinsurers and special purpose vehicles.

The system of solvency assessment under *Solvency II* consists of three pillars:

- Capital requirements (quantitative supervision).
- The process of supervisory analysis (qualified supervision).
- Market discipline (transparency).

The first pillar (quantitative supervision) refers to capital issues and determines minimum financial requirements in quantitative terms. The second (qualified supervision) is designed to improve internal control in an insurance company and the standard of risk management, thus focussing on supervisory processes, and matches the unique nature of a specific insurance company. Defining some shared instruments of prudential supervision, including the harmonisation and standardisation of early warning ratios and the standardisation of control procedures applied by national supervisory authorities, is an important part of the second pillar. The purpose of pillar two (transparency) is to set standard requirements regarding the transparency of actions taken by an insurance company in order to enhance transparency in its insurance company by creating certain information principles. Two types of information published by an insurance company are highlighted: financial information for investors, with the principles of its presentation laid down in the *International Financial Reporting Standard (IFRS)*, and information addressed to the insured.

The system of solvency assessment under the directive concentrates on tying of capital requirements to real risk an entity engaged in insurance activities is exposed to. The capital requirements that form the system encompass:

- *Solvency Capital Requirement (SCR),* which corresponds to allowed equity enabling an insurance company to cover substantial, unexpected losses and to protect the interests of the insured, beneficiaries under the effective contracts of insurance, and assignors under reinsurance treaties.
- *Minimum Capital Requirement (MCR),* the value of allowed equity. Where the insurance company fails to reach the MCR and is unable to generate the equity to meet the minimum capital requirement soon, it should forfeit its insurance licence.

It should be noted that as a result of the introduction of *Solvency II*, insurance companies active in the EU have been bound to maintain two separate reporting systems – one for the purposes of balance sheet regulation and one for the solvency assessment. As required by the directive, insurance and reinsurance companies are bound to draft solvency reports and disclose them to the public. Insurance and reinsurance companies should expect some major changes in this respect following the introduction of the IFRS 17 *Insurance contracts*. In line with the regulations in place, IFRS 17 applies to annual reporting periods starting from 1 January 2023 or later. The principal objective of the standard is to supply more real (market) information about the financial standing and profitability of insurance companies in order to improve the transparency and comparability of financial information presented by insurance companies.

On 22 September 2021, the European Commission published some proposed changes to *Solvency II* (EIOPA, 2021. *Proposal for a directive of the European Parliament and of the Council amending Directive 2009/138/EC as regards proportionality, quality of supervision, reporting, long-term guarantee measures, macro-prudential tools, sustainability risks, group and cross-border supervision*) and a legislative motion for a new directive on the repair, restructuring and orderly liquidation of insurance companies (EIOPA, 2021. *Proposal for a directive of the European Parliament and of the Council establishing a framework for the recovery and resolution of insurance and reinsurance undertakings and amending Directives 2002/47/EC, 2004/25/EC, 2009/138/EC, (EU) 2017/1132 and Regulations (EU) No. 1094/2010 and (EU) No. 648/2012*). The principal objective of the European Commission's efforts is to guide considerable investments of insurance companies towards a rebuilding of Europe after the COVID-19 pandemic, long-term infrastructure investments and a switch to a green and sustainable economy. This means that the legal regulations concerning the insurance market in the EU are subject to regular reviews and adapted to the changing socio-economic reality. It should also be pointed out that the European insurance market is in a good financial condition in spite of the dynamically changing environment and conditions of insurance activities. This is corroborated by EIOPA's stress tests (EIOPA, 2021, *Insurance stress test report*). The regular insurance stress tests are to assess the readiness of the European insurance sector for the likely risk of the financial system. Forty-three insurance groups and one solo insurer took part in the testing, that is, approximately 75% of the insurance sector in the European Economic Area by the value of assets. An assessment of the COVID-19 pandemic's effect on the capital positions and solvency of insurance companies was a special purpose of the 2021 stress test. Its results affirm that the European insurance companies maintain a good financial standing even in hard economic conditions. Similar research was undertaken by the IAIS (*Global Insurance Market Report*, 2021) with regard to the global market. Key risks and trends faced by the global insurance sector identified in the Global Monitoring Exercise (IAIS, *Global Monitoring Exercise*, 2021) are a low-yield environment and the related growth in private equity ownership of insurers, an increased credit risk and heightened cyber risk (IAIS, *Global Insurance Market Report*, 2021).

Conclusions

Ensuring the stability of the insurance market is a major reason for the emergence of the single market. This is bolstered with a range of legal regulations concerning its operation, connected in particular to the solvency assessment. The stability of the financial system is the lack of interferences with its functioning or the achievement of a continuing and dynamic equilibrium in interconnected financial markets (see Solorz, 2001, p. 184). A. Crockett (1997, p. 9) refers financial stability to both institutions and the market, which means that he understands the concept as the stability of key institutions and the market that make up the financial system. Financial stability is reached where:

- Key financial institutions are stable, meaning a high level of confidence they are able to meet their contract liabilities without interruptions or external aid.
- Key markets are stable, meaning the participants can confidently enter into transactions at prices that reflect the fundamental value and are not subject to short-term fluctuations without any fundamental reasons.

A stable financial system works, remains stable in case of far-reaching changes of market conditions and has three key characteristics (International Monetary Fund – IMF, 1997):

- It's flexible – capable of continuing to allocate financial resources in line with the rules of economic effectiveness even in a rapidly changing market environment.
- It's vigorous – the market continues its activities and the transactions are fast and reliable even in case of economic disturbances.
- It's internally consistent – it doesn't by itself generate financial disturbances or escalate internal shocks that could lead to financial crises.

These are the conditions for a stable financial system (see Kiedrowska and Marszałek, 2002, p. 23):

- On the macro scale – a stabilising economic policy, or consistent instruments of monetary and fiscal policies, a well-prepared and sequential financial liberalisation.
- On the macro scale – an appropriate structure and good operation of the market or a "healthy" legal framework, reliability and transparency – appropriate principles of accounting and information disclosure, due management and supervision by owners, effective supervision and auditing, market discipline, an appropriate safety net.

The macro stability means above all healthy economic foundations that can be provided by a state's macroeconomic policy that aims for a balanced rate of economic growth. An appropriately persistent realisation of monetary policy goals, in particular, stable price levels, an extremely important stimulus for long-term contracts, is necessary as well.

Financial stability is undoubtedly a condition of the operation of financial markets, including the insurance market. A financial safety net is a major element assuring its realisation, as it comprises both supervisory (legal) and institutional regulations. It is noteworthy that these issues have been raised by specialist insurance literature virtually always as the concept of the reality of insurance protection, about which Pokorzyński (1957, p. 15) wrote: "insurance stands and falls on the reality of insurance protection" and Szpunar (1978, p. 8) that "it is a necessary characteristic of insurance, without which the insurance not only couldn't properly discharge its various functions, would not only cease to make sense to the insured, but would also turn from a fully reasonable and highly useful institution into something rather harmful", which should be interpreted as a groundless functioning of insurance services that fail to cover the insured losses. The realisation of the principle of reality of insurance protection, like financial stability, should be assured in respect of its internal and external determinants, that is, both with the internal conditions of an insurance company's financial economics and by providing legal regulations and appropriate external structures that guard the financial security of insurance companies, i.e., an appropriate net of financial safety. The single insurance market in the EU undoubtedly bolsters these assurances and contributes to an improved safety of the EU insurance markets.

Notes

1. Shocks specific to a given economy or industry.
2. See more on the FSAP (Pilecka, 2009; Kowalak, 2006, p. 107).
3. The capital requirements for banks and investment firms arising from the New Capital Accord were introduced to the legal order of the European Union with Directives 2006/48/EC and 2006/49/EC. They became effective as of 1 January 2007, with the provisions on the principles of setting the capital requirements entering into force on 1 January 2008; Directive 2006/48/EC relating to the taking up and pursuit of the business of credit institutions; Directive 2006/49/EC of the European Parliament and of the Council of 14 June 2006 on the capital adequacy of investment firms and credit institutions; the Commission Directive 2009/83/EC of 27 July 2009 amending certain Annexes to Directive 2006/48/EC of the European Parliament and of the Council as regards technical provisions concerning risk management – the amendments relate to the technical conditions of the capital requirement due to credit and operational risk; Directive 2009/111/EC of the European Parliament and of the Council of 16 September 2009 amending Directives 2006/48/EC, 2006/49/EC and 2007/64/EC as regards banks affiliated to central institutions, certain own funds items, large exposures, supervisory arrangements and crisis management – the changes relate to the organisation of supervision over European banking groups and additional instruments that can be classified as basic equity; the

Commission Directive 2009/27/EC of 7 April 2009 amending certain Annexes to Directive 2006/49/EC of the European Parliament and of the Council as regards technical provisions concerning risk management – the changes concern the treatment of credit derivative instruments; Directive 2002/87/EC of the European Parliament and of the Council of 16 December 2002 on the supplementary supervision of credit institutions, insurance undertakings and investment firms in a financial conglomerate and amending Council Directives 73/239/EEC, 79/267/EEC, 92/49/EEC, 92/96/EEC, 93/6/EEC and 93/22/EEC, and Directives 98/78/EC and 2000/12/EC of the European Parliament and of the Council. Cf. www.knf.gov.pl.

4. Directive 2002/87/EC of the European Parliament and of the Council of 16 December 2002 on the supplementary supervision of credit institutions, insurance undertakings and investment firms in a financial conglomerate and amending Council Directives 73/239/EEC, 79/267/EEC, 92/49/EEC, 92/96/EEC, 93/6/EEC and 93/22/EEC, and Directives 98/78/EC and 2000/12/EC of the European Parliament and of the Council; Directive 2008/25/EC of the European Parliament and of the Council of 11 March 2008 amending Directive 2002/87/EC on the supplementary supervision of credit institutions, insurance undertakings and investment firms in a financial conglomerate, as regards the implementing powers conferred on the Commission; Directive 2010/78/EU of the European Parliament and of the Council of 24 November 2010 amending Directives 98/26/EC, 2002/87/EC, 2003/6/EC, 2003/41/EC, 2003/71/EC, 2004/39/EC, 2004/109/EC, 2005/60/EC, 2006/48/EC, 2006/49/EC and 2009/65/EC in respect of the powers of the European Supervisory Authority (European Banking Authority), the European Supervisory Authority (European Insurance and Occupational Pensions Authority) and the European Supervisory Authority (European Securities and Markets Authority); cf. www.knf.gov.pl.
5. See more in the European laws cited earlier and Iwanicz-Drozdowska (2009, pp. 161–180).
6. The MIFID was introduced and then modified by force of the following laws: Directive 2004/39/EC of the European Parliament and of the Council of 21 April 2004 on markets in financial instruments amending Council Directives 85/611/EEC and 93/6/EEC and Directive 2000/12/EC of the European Parliament and of the Council and repealing Council Directive 93/22/EEC – MiFID; the (EC) Commission Regulation (EC) No. 1287/2006 of 10 August 2006 implementing Directive 2004/39/EC of the European Parliament and of the Council as regards record-keeping obligations for investment firms, transaction reporting, market transparency, admission of financial instruments to trading and defined terms for the purposes of that Directive; the Commission Directive 2006/73/EC of 10 August 2006 implementing Directive 2004/39/EC of the European Parliament and of the Council as regards organisational requirements and operating conditions for investment firms and defined terms for the purposes of that Directive (the so-called Tier 2 MiFID); Directive 2006/31/EC of the European Parliament and of the Council of 5 April 2006 amending Directive 2004/39/EC on markets in financial instruments, as regards certain deadlines. Cf. www.knf.gov.pl.
7. This is governed by the following directives: Directive 2003/71/EC of the European Parliament and of the Council of 4 November 2003, Directive 2004/109/WE of the European Parliament and of the Council of 15 December 2004 on the harmonisation of transparency requirements in relation to information about issuers whose securities are admitted to trading on a regulated market and amending Directive 2001/34/EC on the prospectus to be published in connection with a public offering or the admission of securities to official stock exchange listing and amending Directive 2001/34/WE; see www.knf.gov.pl.

8. Directive 2008/26/EC of the European Parliament and the Council of 11 March 2008 amending Directive 2003/6/EC on insider dealing and market manipulation (market abuse) in reference to the executive powers conferred on the Commission; Directive 2003/6/EC of the European Parliament and of the Council of 28 January 2003 on insider dealing and market manipulation (market abuse); Commission Directive 2003/124/EC of 22 December 2003 implementing Directive 2003/6/EC of the European Parliament and of the Council as regards the definition and public disclosure of inside information and the definition of market manipulation; Commission Regulation (EC) 2273/2003 of 22 December 2003 implementing Directive 2003/6/EC of the European Parliament and of the Council as regards exemptions for buy-back programmes and stabilisation of financial instruments; the Commission Directive 2004/72/EC of 29 April 2004 implementing Directive 2003/6/EC of the European Parliament and of the Council as regards accepted market practices, the definition of inside information in relation to derivatives on commodities, the drawing up of lists of insiders, the notification of managers' transactions and the notification of suspicious transactions. Cf. www.knf.gov.pl.
9. The Council Directive of 20 December 1985 on the coordination of laws, regulations and administrative provisions relating to undertakings for collective investment in transferable securities (UCITS III); Directive 2009/65/EC of the European Parliament and of the Council of 13 July 2009 on the coordination of laws, regulations and administrative provisions relating to undertakings for collective investment in transferable securities (UCITS IV); cf. www.knf.gov.pl.
10. The Commission Regulation (EC) No. 1126/2008 of 3 November 2008 adopting certain international accounting standards in accordance with Regulation (EC) No. 1606/2002 of the European Parliament and of the Council; Regulation (EC) No. 297/2008 of the European Parliament and of the Council of 11 March 2008 amending Regulation (EC) No. 1606/2002 on the application of international accounting standards, as regards the implementing powers conferred on the Commission; Regulation (EC) No. 1606/2002 of the European Parliament and of the Council of 19 July 2002 on the application of international accounting standards; the International Standards of Accounting; the approval process of the International Standards of Accounting (ISA) in the European Union; the International Standards of Financial Reporting, Interpretations by KIMSF (the Committee for the Interpretation of the International Standards of Financial Reporting) and SKI (Standing Interpretation Committee); cf. www.knf.gov.pl.
11. See the following EU laws at www.knf.gov.pl: 2007/601/EC: Decision of the European Central Bank of 24 July 2007 concerning the terms and conditions of TARGET2-EBC (EBC/2007/7) TARGET2 – Trans European Automated Real Time Gross Settlement Express Transfer; 2009/338/EC: Decision of the European Central Bank of 19 March 2009 concerning the establishment of the (TARGET2-Securities Programme Board (EBC/2009/6)).
12. Read more on the progress of legislative work in *Postęp prac nad utworzeniem nowej architektury nadzoru finansowego w UE*, www.nbp.gov.pl.
13. LCR is the relation of highly liquid assets to total outgoing cash in a bank in the next 30 calendar days. It should be at least 100%.
14. NSFR is defined as the available stable financing funds divided by the required amount of stable financing. Its design is based on the concept of net liquid assets. The required amount of financing is referred to all non-liquid assets and securities held, as well as a small portion of liabilities resulting from off-balance liabilities. The NSFR of a bank must be above 100%.
15. Where an insurance company is part of a group, the amount of the whole group's technical reserves is taken into account.

Bibliography

Allen, F. & Gale, D., 2001. *Comparing Financial Systems*. London: The MIT Press.

Allen, F. & Santomero, A. M., 1997. The theory of financial intermediation. *Journal of Banking and Finance*, 21, pp. 1461–1486.

Arcand, J. L., Berkes, E. & Panizza, U., 2012. Too Much Finance? IMF Working Paper, No. 161.

Arrow, J. K., 1951. An extension of the basic theorem of classical welfare economics. In: Neyman J. (Ed.), *Proceedings of the Second Berkeley Symposium in Mathematical Statistics and Probability*, Berkeley: University of California Press, pp. 507–532.

Arrow, J. K., 1964. The role of securities in optimal allocation of risk – Bearing. *Review of Economic Studies*, 31, pp. 91–96.

Baily, M. N. & Lawrance, R. Z., 2001. Do we have a new economy? *The American Economic Review*, 91 (2), pp. 308–312.

BCBS, 2011. *Basel III: A Global Regulatory Framework for More Resilient Banks and Banking System – Revised Version*. Basel: BIS.

BCBS, 2013. *Basel III: The Liquidity Coverage Ratio and Liquidity Coverage Ratio and Liquidity Risk Monitoring Tools*. Basel: BIS.

Beck, T., 2013. Finance, growth and fragility: The role for government. *International Journal of Banking. Accounting and Finance*, 5 (1/2), pp. 49–70.

Beck, T., Levine, R. & Loyaza, N., 2000. Financial intermediation and growth: Causality and causes. *Journal of Monetary Economics*, 46, pp. 31–77.

Bijak, W., 2003. Zewnętrzna ocena zakładu ubezpieczeń, In: Monkiewicz, J. (Ed.), *Podstawy ubezpieczeń – przedsiębiorstwo*, Warszawa: Poltext.

Bijak, W., 2009. *Praktyczne metody badania niewypłacalności zakładu ubezpieczeń*. Warszawa: SGH.

Bukowski, S. I., 2020. *Financial Integration in the European Monetary Union*. New York; London: Routledge, Taylor & Francis Group.

Bukowski, S. I., 2011. Economic monetary union – Current fiscal disturbances and the future. *International Advances in Economic Research*, An Official Publication of the International Atlantic Economic Society, 17 (3), pp. 274–287.

Bukowski, S. I., 2011. *Międzynarodowa integracja rynków finansowych*. Warszawa: Difin.

Bukowski, S. I., 2013, *Integracja rynków finansowych w Unii europejskiej. Czechy, Polska, Słowacja, Słowenia, Węgry – obszar euro*. Radom: Spatium, pp. 65–72.

Caporale, G. M., Howells, P. G. A. & Soliman, A. M., 2004. Stock market development and economic growth: The causal linkage. *Journal of Economic Development*, 29 (1), pp. 33–50.

Caporale, G. M., Howells, P. G. A. & Soliman, A. M., 2005. Endogenous growth models and stock market development: Evidence from four countries. *Review of Development Economics*, 9 (2), pp. 166–176.

Carré, E. & L'œillet, G., 2018. The literature on finance-growth nexus in the aftermath of the financial crisis: A review. *Comparative Economic Studies*, 60 (1), pp. 161–180.

Cecchetti, S. & Kharroubi, E., 2012. Reassessing the impact of finance on growth, *BIS Working Paper*, 381.

Cline, W., 2015. Too much finance, or statistical illusion? *Policy Brief*, 1 (1), pp. 1–6.

Commission Directive 2003/124/EC of 22 December 2003 implementing Directive 2003/6/EC of the European Parliament and of the Council as regards the definition and public disclosure of inside information and the definition of market manipulation, Official Journal of the European Communities on 24.12.2003, No. L 339.

Commission Directive 2004/72/EC of 29 April 2004 implementing Directive 2003/6/EC of the European Parliament and of the Council as regards accepted market practices, the definition of inside information in relation to derivatives on commodities, the drawing up of lists of insiders, the notification of managers' transactions and the notification of suspicious transactions, Official Journal of the European Communities on 30.4.2004, No. L 162.

Commission Directive 2006/73/EC of 10 August 2006 implementing Directive 2004/39/EC of the European Parliament and of the Council as regards organisational requirements and operating conditions for investment firms and defined terms for the purposes of that Directive, Official Journal of the European Communities on 2.9.2006, No. L 241.

Commission Directive 2009/27/EC of 7 April 2009 amending certain Annexes to Directive 2006/49/EC of the European Parliament and of the Council as regards technical provisions concerning risk management, Official Journal of the European Communities on 8.4.2009, No. L 94.

Commission Directive 2009/83/EC of 27 July 2009 amending certain Annexes to Directive 2006/48/EC of the European Parliament and of the Council as regards technical provisions concerning risk management, Official Journal of the European Communities on 28.7.2009, No. L 196.

Commission Regulation (EC) No. 1126/2008 of 3 November 2008 adopting certain international accounting standards in accordance with Regulation (EC) No. 1606/2002 of the European Parliament and of the Council, Official Journal of the European Communities on 29.11.2008, No. L 320.

Commission Regulation (EC) No. 1287/2006 of 10 August 2006 implementing Directive 2004/39/EC of the European Parliament and of the Council as regards record-keeping obligations for investment firms, transaction reporting, market transparency, admission of financial instruments to trading, and defined terms for the purposes of that Directive, Official Journal of the European Communities on 2.9.2006, No. L 241.

Commission Regulation (EC) No. 2273/2003 of 22 December 2003 implementing Directive 2003/6/EC of the European Parliament and of the Council as regards exemptions for buy-back programmes and stabilisation of financial instruments, Official Journal of the European Communities on 23.12.2003, No. L 336.

Conant, S., Desoutler, N. L., Long, D. L. & Macgrogan, R., 1996. *Managing for Solvency and Profitability in Life and Health Insurance Companies*. Atlanta: LOMA.

Council Directive 85/611/EEC of 20 December 1985 on the coordination of laws, regulations and administrative provisions relating to undertakings for collective investment in transferable securities (UCITS), Official Journal of the European Communities on 31.12.1985, No. L 375.

Council Directive 90/619/EEC of 8 November 1990 on the coordination of laws, regulations and administrative provisions relating to direct life assurance, laying down provisions to facilitate the effective exercise of freedom to provide services and amending Directive 79/267/EEC. Official Journal of the European Communities on 29.11.90, No. L 330/50.

Council Directive 92/49/EEC of 18 June 1992 on the coordination of laws, regulations and administrative provisions relating to direct insurance other than life assurance and amending Directives 73/239/EEC and 88/357/EEC (third non-life insurance Directive). Official Journal of the European Communities on 11.8.92, No. L 228/1.

Council Directive 92/96/EEC of 10 November 1992 on the coordination of laws, regulations and administrative provisions relating to direct life assurance and amending Directives 79/267/EEC and 90/619/EEC (third life assurance Directive). Official Journal of the European Communities on 9.12.92, No. L 360/1.

Council Directive 93/22/EEC of 10 May 1993 on investment services in the securities field, Official Journal of the European Communities on 11.6.1993, No. L 141.

Coutts, S. M. & Devit, S., 1989. The assessment of the financial strength of insurance companies, by a generalized cash flow model, In: Cummins, J. D. & Derrig, R. A. (Eds.), *Financial Models of Insurance Solvency*, Boston-Dordrecht-London: Kluwer Publishers.

Crockett, A., 1997. Why is financial stability a goal of public policy?, In: *Maintaining Financial Stability in a Global Economy*, Symposium Series. Kansas City: Federal Reserve Bank of Kansas City.

de Larosiere, J., 2009. *Report.* 25 February, Brussels: The High – Level Group on Financial Supervision in the EU chaired by Jacques de Larosiere.

Debreu, G., 1959. *Theory of Value.* New York: Willey.

Dębski, W., 2003. *Rynek finansowy i jego mechanizmy. Podstawy teorii i praktyki.* Warszawa: PWN.

Dębski, W., Maciejczyk, I. & Wdowinski, P., 2010. Growth effects of financial market development in Poland: Simulations with an econometric model. In: Bukowski, S. I. (Ed.), *Global Challenges of the 21th Century*, Radom: Technical University of Radom, Publishing Office, pp. 361–398.

Decision ECB/2007/7. Decision of the European Central Bank of 24 July 2007 concerning the terms and conditions of TARGET2-ECB (ECB/2007/7), Official Journal of the European Communities on 8.9.2007, No. L 237.

Decision ECB/2009/6. Decision of the ECB of 29 March 2012 on the establishment of the TARGET2-Securities Board and repealing (ECB/2012/6), Official Journal of the European Communities on 1.5.2012, No. L 117.

Diamond, D. W. & Dybvig, P. H., 1983. Bank runs, deposit insurance, and liquidity. *The Journal of Political Economy*, 91 (3), pp. 401–419.

Directive (EU) 2019/2161 of the European Parliament and of the Council of 27 November 2019 amending Council Directive 93/13/EEC and Directives 98/6/EC, 2005/29/EC and 2011/83/EU of the European Parliament and of the Council as regards the better enforcement and modernisation of Union consumer protection rules. Official Journal of the European Communities on 18.12.2019, No. L 328/7.

Directive 2000/12/EC of the European Parliament and of the Council of 20 March 2000 relating to the taking up and pursuit of the business of credit institutions, Official Journal of the European Communities on 26.5.2000, No. L 126.

Directive 2002/87/EC of the European Parliament and of the Council of 16 December 2002 on the supplementary supervision of credit institutions, insurance undertakings and investment firms in a financial conglomerate and amending Council Directives 73/239/EEC, 79/267/EEC, 92/49/EEC, 92/96/EEC, 93/6/EEC and 93/22/EEC, and Directives 98/78/EC and 2000/12/EC of the European Parliament and of the Council, Official Journal of the European Communities on 11.2.2003, No. L 35.

Directive 2003/6/EC of the European Parliament and of the Council of 28 January 2003 on insider dealing and market manipulation (market abuse), Official Journal of the European Communities on 12.4.2003, No. L 96.

Directive 2003/71/EC of the European Parliament and of the Council of 4 November 2003 on the prospectus to be published when securities are offered to the public or admitted to trading and amending Directive 2001/34/EC, Official Journal of the European Communities on 31.12.2003, No. L 345.
Directive 2004/109/EC of the European Parliament and of the Council of 15 December 2004 on the harmonisation of transparency requirements in relation to information about issuers whose securities are admitted to trading on a regulated market and amending Directive 2001/34/EC, Official Journal of the European Communities on 31.12.2004, No. L 390.
Directive 2004/39/EC of the European Parliament and of the Council of 21 April 2004 on markets in financial instruments amending Council Directives 85/611/EEC and 93/6/EEC and Directive 2000/12/EC of the European Parliament and of the Council and repealing Council Directive 93/22/EEC, Official Journal of the European Communities on 30.4.2004, No. L 145.
Directive 2005/1/EC of the European Parliament and of the Council of 9 March 2005 amending Council Directives 73/239/EEC, 85/611/EEC, 91/675/EEC, 92/49/EEC and 93/6/EEC and Directives 94/19/EC, 98/78/EC, 2000/12/EC, 2001/34/EC, 2002/83/EC and 2002/87/EC in order to establish a new organisational structure for financial services committees, Official Journal of the European Communities on 24.3.2005, No. L 79.
Directive 2006/31/EC of the European Parliament and of the Council of 5 April 2006 amending directive 2004/39/EC on markets in financial instruments, as regards certain deadlines, Official Journal of the European Communities on 27.4.2006, No. L 114.
Directive 2006/48/EC of the European Parliament and of the Council of 14 June 2006 relating to the taking up and pursuit of the business of credit institutions, Official Journal of the European Communities on 30.6.2006, No. L 177.
Directive 2006/49/EC of the European Parliament and of the Council of 14 June 2006 on the capital adequacy of investment firms and credit institutions, Official Journal of the European Communities on 30.6.2006, No. L 177.
Directive 2008/25/EC of the European Parliament and of the Council of 11 March 2008 amending Directive 2002/87/EC on the supplementary supervision of credit institutions, insurance undertakings and investment firms in a financial conglomerate, as regards the implementing powers conferred on the Commission, Official Journal of the European Communities on 20.3.2008, No. L 81.
Directive 2008/26/EC of the European Parliament and of the Council of 11 March 2008 amending Directive 2003/6/EC on insider dealing and market manipulation (market abuse), as regards the implementing powers conferred on the Commission, Official Journal of the European Communities on 20.3.2008, No. L 81.
Directive 2009/111/EC of the European Parliament and of the Council of 16 September 2009 amending Directives 2006/48/EC, 2006/49/EC and 2007/64/EC as regards banks affiliated to central institutions, certain own funds items, large exposures, supervisory arrangements, and crisis management, Official Journal of the European Communities on 17.11.2009, No. L 302.
Directive 2009/138/EC of the European Parliament and of the Council of 25 November 2009 on the taking-up and pursuit of the business of insurance and reinsurance (Solvency II). Official Journal of the European Communities on 23.12.2009, No. L 335/1.

Directive 2009/65/EC of the European Parliament and of the Council of 13 July 2009 on the coordination of laws, regulations and administrative provisions relating to undertakings for collective investment in transferable securities (UCITS), Official Journal of the European Communities on 17.11.2009, No. L 302.

Directive 2010/78/EU of the European Parliament and of the Council of 24 November 2010 amending Directives 98/26/EC, 2002/87/EC, 2003/6/EC, 2003/41/EC, 2003/71/EC, 2004/39/EC, 2004/109/EC, 2005/60/EC, 2006/48/EC, 2006/49/EC and 2009/65/EC in respect of the powers of the European Supervisory Authority (European Banking Authority), the European Supervisory Authority (European Insurance and Occupational Pensions Authority) and the European Supervisory Authority (European Securities and Markets Authority), Official Journal of the European Communities on 15.12.2010, No. L 331.

Directive 2013/36/EU of the European Parliament and of the Council of 26 June 2013 on access to the activity of credit institutions and the prudential supervision of credit institutions and investment firms, amending Directive 2002/87/EC and repealing Directives 2006/48/EC and 2006/49/EC, Official Journal of the European Communities on 27.6.2013, No. L 176.

Directive Omnibus I – Directive (EU) No. 2010/78/EU of the European Parliament and of the Council of 24 November 2010 amending Directive 98/26/EC, 2002/87/EC, 2003/6/EC, 2003/41/EC, 2003/71/EC, 2004/39/EC, 2004/109/EC, 2005/60/EC, 2006/48/EC, 2006/49/EC, 2009/65/EC as regards the powers of the European Supervisory Authority (European Banking Authority), the European Supervisory Authority (European Insurance and Occupational Pensions Authority) and the European Supervisory Authority (European Securities and Markets Authority).

Directive Omnibus II – Directive of the European Parliament and of the Council (EU) amending Directives 2003/71/EC and 2009/138/EC as regards the powers of the European Insurance and Occupational Pensions Authority and the European Securities and Markets Authority (COD 2011/0006).

Doumbia, D., 2016. Financial development and economic growth in 43 advanced and developing economies over the period 1975–2009: Evidence of non-linearity. *Applied Econometrics and International Development*, 1, pp. 13–22.

EC, 1999. Communication from the commission – implementing the framework for financial markets: Action plan, COM(1999) 232, 11.05.1999.

EC, 2004. EMU after five years. European Economy, Special Report No. 1.

ECB, 2019a. Financial integration indicators. Retrieved from https://sdw.ecb.europa.eu/browse.do?node=9691128 on May 15, 2019.

ECB, 2019b. Indicators of financial integration in the euro area. Retrieved from https://www.ecb.europa.eu/stats/financial_markets_and_interest_rates/financial_integration/html/index.en.html on May 15, 2019.

EIOPA, 2021. Insurance stress test report. 16 December 2021, Frankfurt am Main: European Insurance and Occupational Pensions Authority.

EIOPA, 2021. *Proposal for a directive of the European Parliament and of the Council amending Directive 2009/138/EC as regards proportionality, quality of supervision, reporting, long-term guarantee measures, macro-prudential tools, sustainability risks, group and cross-border supervision*. 22 September 2021. Retrieved from https://eur-lex.europa.eu/legal-content/EN/TXT/?uri=CELEX:52021PC0581on September 22, 2021.

EIOPA, 2021. *Proposal for a directive of the European Parliament and of the Council establishing a framework for the recovery and resolution of insurance and reinsurance undertakings and amending Directives 2002/47/EC, 2004/25/EC, 2009/138/ EC, (EU) 2017/1132 and Regulations (EU) No. 1094/2010 and (EU) No. 648/201222*. September 2021. Retrieved from https://eur-lex.europa.eu/legal-content/EN/TXT/?uri=CELEX%3A52021PC0582 on September 15, 2021.

Eschenbach, F. & Francois, J. F., 2005. *Finance and growth: A synthesis of trade and investment related transmission mechanisms*, Retrieved from http://citeseerx.ist.psu.edu/viewdoc/download?doi=10.1.1.114.8518&rep=rep1&type=pdf on July 12, 2018.

Euphasio, J. W. & Carvalho, J. V. F., 2020. *Reinsurance and solvency capital: Mitigating insurance companies' ruin probability*. Retrieved from https://doi.org/10.1590/1982-7849rac2022200191.en on January 15, 2022.

Fiedor, B., 1979. *Teoria innowacji. Krytyczna analiza współczesnych koncepcji niemarksistowskich*. Warszawa: PWN.

First Council Directive 73/239/EEC of 24 July 1973 on the coordination of laws, regulations and administrative provisions relating to the taking-up and pursuit of the business of direct insurance other than life assurance. Official Journal of the European Communities on 16.8.73, No. L 228/3.

First Council Directive 79/267/EEC of 5 March 1979 on the coordination of laws, regulations and administrative provisions relating to the taking up and pursuit of the business of direct life assurance. Official Journal of the European Communities on 13.3.79, No. L 63/1.

Flejterski, S., 2011. Banki jako współsprawcy i współbeneficjenci globalnego kryzysu finansowego. In: Bednarczyk, J. L. & Przybylska-Kapuścińska, W. (Eds.), *Od kryzysu do ożywienia. Dylematy współczesnej polityki finansowej*, Warszawa: CeDeWu.pl Wydawnictwa Fachowe, pp. 103–118.

Giannetti, M., Guiso, L., Japelli, T., Padula, M. & Pagano, M., 2002. Financial Market Integration, Corporate Financing and Economic Growth. Final Report (22 November). *European Economy: Economic Papers*, No. 179, November.

Greenwood, J. & Jovanovic, B., 1989. Financial Development, Growth, and the Distribution of Income, *NBER Working Paper*, No. 3189, December.

Hardie, A. C., Limb, A. P., Loades, D. H., Lumsden, K., Mason, D. C., Pollock, G., Robertson, W. F., Scott, W. F. & Wilkie, A. D., 1986. The solvency of life assurance companies, *Transactions of the Faculty of Actuaries*, 38, pp. 253–269.

Horvath, R., 2017. Financial market fragmentation and monetary transmission in the euro area: What do we know? *Journal of Economic Policy Reform*, 21 (4), pp. 319–334.

Hyz, A. & Gikas, G., 2018. Financial system supervision: Towards the European Banking union. In: Bukowski, S. I. (Ed.), *Monetary Unions. Backgrounds, Advantages and Disadvantages*, New York: Nova Science Publishers, Inc.

IAIS, 2000. *On Solvency, Solvency Assessment and Actuarial Issues*. Basel: International Association of Insurance Supervisors.

IAIS, 2021. *Global Insurance Market Report*. Basel: International Association of Insurance Supervisors.

IAIS, 2021. *Global Monitoring Exercise (GME) Highlights Key Financial Stability Priorities for Insurance Supervisors*. Basel: International Association of Insurance Supervisors.

IFRS 17 Insurance contracts. Commission Regulation (EU) 2021/2036 of 19 November 2021 amending Regulation (EC) No. 1126/2008 adopting certain international accounting standards in accordance with Regulation (EC) No. 1606/2002 of the European Parliament and of the Council as regards International Financial Reporting Standard 17. Official Journal of the European Communities on 23.11.2021, No. L 416/6.

IMF. 1997. *Financial Stability in Emerging Market Economies. A Strategy for Formulation Adoption and Implementation of Sound Principles and Practices to Strengthen Financial System*, Report of the Working Party on Financial Stability in Emerging Market Economies, Bank for International Settlement – International Monetary Fund, Basel 1997.

Iwanicz-Drozdowska, M., 2009. Konglomeraty finansowe. In: Iwanicz-Drozdowska, M. (Ed.), *Integracja rynków finansowych w Unii Europejskiej od A do Z*, Warszawa: NBP, pp. 161–180.

Janicka, M., 2005. Jednolity rynek finansowy Unii Europejskiej – początek kolejnego etapu – "Zielona Księga". *Bank i Kredyt*, 9, pp. 42–53.

Kahane, Y., Tapiero, C. C. & Jacques, L., 1989. Concept and trends in the study of insurer's solvency, In: Cummins, J. D. & Dering, R. A. (Eds.), *Financial Models of Insurance Solvency*, Boston-Correct-London: Lower Academic Publishers.

Kasperkiewicz, W., 2009. Obecny kryzys finansowy – przyczyny i terapia. In: Bednarczyk, J. L., Bukowski, S. I. & Misala, J. (Eds.), *Współczesny kryzys gospodarczy. Przyczyny- przebieg- skutki*, Warszawa: CeDeWu, pp. 33–44.

Kastelijn, W. M. & Remmerswaal, J. C. M., 1986. *Solvency. Surveys of Actuarial Studies*. Rotterdam: Nationale Nederlanden.

Kiedrowska, M. & Marszałek, P. 2002. Stabilność finansowa – pojęcie, cechy i sposoby jej zapewnienia. *Bank Kredyt*, 3, pp. 21–28.

King, R. & Levine, R., 1993. Finance and growth: Schumpeter might be right. *Quarterly Journal of Economics*, 108 (3), pp. 717–737.

KNF, 2019. *Regulacje i dokumenty powiązane*. Retrieved from https://www.knf.gov.pl/o_nas/wspolpraca_miedzynarodowa/unia/regulacje_UE_i_dokumenty_powiazane on May 15, 2019.

Kowalak, T., 2006. *Integracja rynków kapitałowych w Unii Europejskiej*. Warszawa: TWIGGER.

Lament, M., 2013. *Ocena wypłacalności zakładu ubezpieczeń a system informacyjny rachunkowości*. Warszawa: CeDeWu.

Łazowski, J., 1934. *Wstęp do nauki o ubezpieczeniach*. Warszawa: PZUW.

Leland, H. E. & Pyle, D. H., 1977. Informational asymmetries, financial structure and financial intermediation. *Journal of Finance*, 32, pp. 371–387.

Levine, R., 1991. Stock markets, growth, and tax policy. *Journal of Finance*, 46, pp. 1445–1465.

Levine, R., 2004. Finance and Growth: Theory and Evidence. *NBER Working Paper*, No. 10766, September.

Levine, R., Loayza, N. & Beck, T., 2000. Financial intermediation and growth: Causality and causes. *Journal of Monetary Economics*, 46, pp. 31–77.

Lisowski, J., 2010. *Specyfika gospodarki finansowej ubezpieczycieli kredytu kupieckiego*. Poznań: Wydawnictwo Uniwersytetu Ekonomicznego w Poznaniu.

Lucas, R., 1988. On mechanism of economic development. *Journal of Monetary Economics*, 22, pp. 3–42.

Maastricht Treaty. European Union 1992. Treaty on European Union. Official Journal of the European Communities on 29. 7. 92, No. C 191/1.

Marcinkowska, M., 2016. Bazylea III i pakiet CRD IV/CRR – Charakterystyka wymogów kapitałowych i płynnościowych. In: Marcinkowska, M. & Wdowiński, P.

(Eds.), *Wpływ regulacji kapitałowych i płynnościowych sektora bankowego na wzrost gospodarczy Polski*, Łódź: Wydawnictwo Uniwersytetu Łódzkiego, pp. 41–92.

Merton, R. C., 1993. Operation and regulation in financial intermediation: A functional perspective. In: P. England (Ed.), *Operation and Regulation of Financial Markets*, Stockholm: The Economic Council, pp. 4–67.

Merton, R. C., 1995. A functional perspective of financial intermediation. *Financial Management*, 24, pp. 23–41.

Merton, R. C. & Bodie, Z., 1995. A conceptual framework for analyzing the financial environment. In: Crane, D. B., Froot, K. A., Mason, S. P., Perold, A., Merton, R. C., Bodie, Z., Sirri, E. R. & Tufano, P. (Eds.), *The Global Financial System: A Functional Perspective*, Boston: Harvard Business School. pp. 3–31.

Miller, M. H., 1998. Financial markets and economic growth. *Journal of Applied Corporate Finance*, 11 (3), pp. 8–15.

Monkiewicz, J. & Monkiewicz, M., 2005. Jednolity rynek finansowy Unii Europejskiej, In: Monkiewicz, J. (Ed.), *Jednolity rynek ubezpieczeń w Unii Europejskiej. Procesy rozwoju i integracji*, Bydgoszcz – Warszawa: Oficyna Wydawnicza Branta, pp. 45–64.

Müllers Report, 1997. Konferenz der Vesicherungsaufsichtsbehorde der Mitglidstaaten der Europaischen Union, Berlin, April 1997.

NBP, 2010. *Postęp prac nad utworzeniem nowej architektury nadzoru finansowego w UE*, Retrieved from https://www.nbp.pl/publikacje/integracja_europejska/nowa_architektura_nadzoru_finansowego_w_ue_postep_prac_07_2010.pdf on May 15, 2015.

Nieborak, T., 2008. *Aspekty prawne funkcjonowania rynku finansowego Unii Europejskiej*. Warszawa: Difin.

Oręziak, L., 1996. Jednolity rynek ubezpieczeniowy w ramach w ramach Unii Europejskiej – zasady funkcjonowania i kierunki rozwoju. *International Journal of Management and Economics*, 1, pp. 36–41.

Osiński, J., Wyczański, P., Tymoczko, D. & Grąt, A., 2004. *Rozwój systemu finansowego w Polsce w latach 2002–2003*. Warszawa: NBP, grudzień.

Outreville, J. F., 1998. *Theory and Practice of Insurance*. Dordrecht; Boston; London: Kluwer Academic Publishers.

Panek, E., 2003. *Ekonomia matematyczna*. Poznań: Wydawnictwo Akademii Ekonomicznej w Poznaniu.

Pantikainen, T., Bonsdorf, H., Pesonen, H., Rantala, J. & Ruohonen, M., 1989. *Insurance Solvency and Financial Strength*. Helsinki: Finnish Insurance Training and Publishing Company.

Petit, P., 2002. The Roots of the New Economy: An Institutional Perspective. CEPREMAP/CNRS, Universite de Paris Sud (XI), May 17–18.

Pietrzak, B. & Polański, Z., 2000. *System finansowy w Polsce. Lata dziewięćdziesiąte*. Warszawa: PWN.

Pilecka, A., 2009. Plan działań w zakresie usług finansowych (FSAP) – założenia, realizacja i wpływ na rynki finansowe w Unii Europejskiej. In: Iwanicz-Drozdowska, M. (Ed.), *Integracja rynków finansowych w Unii Europejskiej od A do Z*, Warszawa: NBP, pp. 25–48.

Pokorzyński, L., 1957. Uwagi w sprawie podstawowych zasad ubezpieczeń w Polsce, *Zeszyty Naukowe Wyższej Szkoły Ekonomicznej w Poznaniu*, 4, pp. 12–19.

Próchniak, M. & Wasiak, K., 2016. Zależność między rozwojem i stabilnością sektora finansowego a tempem wzrostu gospodarczego w krajach Unii Europejskiej ze szczególnym uwzględnieniem państw Europy Środkowo – Wschodniej. *Rocznik Instytutu Europy Środkowo-Wschodniej*, 14 (5), pp. 163–182.

Rajan, R. & Zingales, L., 1996. Financial Dependence and Growth. *NBER Working Paper*, No. 5758.

Regulation (EC) No. 1606/2002 of the European Parliament and of the Council of 19 July 2002 on the application of international accounting standards, Official Journal of the European Communities on 11.9.2002, No. L 243.

Regulation (EC) No. 297/2008 of the European Parliament and of the Council of 11 March 2008 amending Regulation (EC) No. 1606/2002 on the application of international accounting standards, as regards the implementing powers conferred on the Commission, Official Journal of the European Communities on 19.4.2008, No. L 97.

Regulation (EU) No. 575/2013 of the European Parliament and of the Council of 26 June 2013 on prudential requirements for credit institutions and investment firms and amending Regulation (EU) No. 648/2012, Official Journal of the European Communities on 27.6.2013, No. L 176.

Regulation (EU) No. 1092/2010 of the European Parliament and of the Council of 24 November 2010 on Community macroprudential supervision of the financial system and establishing a European Systemic Risk Board.

Regulation (EU) No. 1093/2010 of the European Parliament and of the Council of November 24, 2010 on the establishment of the European Supervisory Authority (European Banking Authority), amending Decision No. 716/2009/EC and repealing Commission Decision 2009/78/EC.

Regulation (EU) No. 1094/2010 of the European Parliament and of the Council of November 24, 2010 on the establishment of the European Supervisory Authority (European Insurance and Occupational Pensions Authority), amending Decision No. 716/2009/EC and repealing Commission Decision 2009/79/EC.

Regulation (EU) No. 1095 of the European Parliament and of the Council 2010 of 24 November 2010 on the establishment of the European Supervisory Authority (European Securities and Markets Authority), changes Decision No. 716/2009/EC and repealing Commission Decision 2009/77/EC.

Robinson, J., 1952. The generalization of the general theory. In: *The Rate of Interest and Other Essays*, London: Macmillan.

Roubini, N. & Sala-Martin, X., 1992. Financial repression and economic growth. *Journal of Development Economics*, 39 (1), pp. 5–30.

Rousseau, P. L. & Wachtel, P., 2005. Economic Growth and Financial Depth: Is the Relationship Extinct Already? *WIDER Discussion Paper*, 2005/10.

Rubin, H. W., 1995. *Dictionary of Insurance Terms*. New York: Barrons Educational Series.

Sandstrom, A., 2006. *Solvency: Models, Assessment and Regulation*. Boca Raton' London; New York: Taylor & Francis Group.

Scholtens, B. & van Wensveen, D., 2003. *The Theory of Financial Intermediation: An Essay on What It Does (Not) Explain*. Vienna: SUERF – The European Money and Finance Forum.

Schumpeter, J., 1960. *Teoria rozwoju gospodarczego*. Warszawa: PWN.

Second Council Directive 88/357/EEC of 22 June 1988 on the coordination of laws, regulations and administrative provisions relating to direct insurance other than life assurance and laying down provisions to facilitate the effective exercise of freedom to provide services and amending Directive 73/239/EEC. Official Journal of the European Communities on 4.7.88, No. L/172/1.

Siri, E. R. & Tufano, P., 1985. *The Global System: A Functional Approach*. Cambridge: Harvard Business School Press.

Solorz, J. K., 2001. *Międzynarodowy system finansowy. Analiza instytucjonalno-porównawcza*. Warszawa: Biblioteka Menedżera i Bankowca.

Stulz, R., 2004. Does financial structure matter for economic growth? A corporate finance perspectives. In: Demirgüç-Kunt, A. & Levine, R. (Eds.), *Financial Structure and Economic Growth. A Cross-Country Comparison of Banks, Markets, and Development*, Cambridge, MA; London: The MIT Press.

Szpunar, J., 1978. Zasada realności ochrony ubezpieczeniowej, *Wiadomości Ubezpieczeniowe*, 8, pp. 7–15.

Treaty of Rome. European Union 2002. Consolidated versions of the Treaty on European Union and of the Treaty establishing the European Community. Official Journal of the European Communities on 24.12.2002, No. C 325/2.

Von Pischke, J. D., 1991. *Finance at the Frontier. Debt Capacity and the Role of Credit in the Private Economy*. New York: Economic Development Institute of The World Bank, The World Bank 9788.

2 The specificity and determinants of the development of international insurance markets

The main segments of the global insurance market – Specificities

The insurance market is a segment of the financial market. For geographical reasons, the global insurance market can be divided into the following major parts:

- North America
- The EU
- Asia

To demonstrate the status and significance of the European insurance market in the global market, Tables 2.1 and 2.2 present the world insurance market by continents in 2010–2020. The market share is measured with written insurance premium. It is presented in general and divided into life insurance and non-life insurance. For the purpose of a more synthetic presentation of changes in the global market, the data concern three periods, i.e., 2010, 2016 and 2020. The division of the global insurance market by regions is illustrated in Figure 2.1 as well.

An analysis of the figures in Tables 2.1 and 2.2 and in Figure 2.1 shows that the share of the European insurance market in the world market has been shrinking. This is true of both life (2010 – 38.3%, 2016 – 33.3%, 2020 – 30.5%) and non-life insurance (2010 –36%, 2016 – 28.9%, 2020 – 19.3%).

Tables 2.3 and 2.4 list the values of written premium divided into the particular national European markets and the shares of the national markets in the European insurance market, thus illustrating the structure of the European insurance market. The premium is divided into life and non-life insurance.

The structure of the European insurance market in 2010–2020 is shown in Figure 2.2, too.

A review of the data in Tables 2.3 and 2.4 and in Figure 2.2 proves that the United Kingdom, France, Italy and Germany are the four largest European

DOI: 10.4324/9781003227762-2

Table 2.1 The world insurance market in 2010–2020 (gross written premium, dollar, million)

Specification	*Total*			*Life insurance*			*Non-life insurance*		
	2010	*2016*	*2020*	*2010*	*2016*	*2020*	*2010*	*2016*	*2020*
Europe	1,620,437	1,470,021	1,540,666	965,661	858,607	886,880	654,775	611,414	653,786
North America	1,281,664	1,466,908	2,674,038	557,802	608,823	690,921	723,861	858,085	1,983,117
Asia	1,161,118	1,453,991	1,701,051	855,370	960,731	1,090,766	305,748	493,260	610,285
Latin America	127,867	148,500	131,854	54,547	69,212	59,938	73,320	79,288	71,916
Oceania	81,160	92,524	195,231	39,448	39,537	141,762	41,713	52,987	53,469
Africa	66,719	60,709	60,190	47,244	40,571	41,097	19,475	20,138	19,093
Total	4,338,964	4,692,653	6,303,030	2,520,072	2,577,481	2,911,364	1,818,892	2,115,172	3,391,666

Source: The authors' own research on the basis of Swiss Re (2011, 2017, 2020, 2021).

Table 2.2 The shares in the world insurance market in 2010–2020 (%)

	Total			*Life insurance*			*Non-life insurance*		
Specification	*2010*	*2016*	*2020*	*2010*	*2016*	*2020*	*2010*	*2016*	*2020*
Europe	37.4	31.1	24.4	38.3	33.3	30.5	36.0	28.9	19.3
North America	29.5	31.0	42.4	22.1	23.6	23.7	39.8	40.6	58.5
Asia	26.7	31.6	27.0	33.9	37.3	37.5	16.8	23.3	18.0
Latin America	3.0	3.1	2.2	2.2	2.7	2.1	4.0	3.7	2.1
Oceania	1.9	2.0	3.1	1.6	1.5	4.8	2.3	2.5	1.6
Africa	1.5	1.3	0.9	1.9	1.6	1.4	1.1	1.0	0.5
Total	100.0	100.0	100.0	100.0	100.0	100.0	100.0	100.0	100.0

Source: The authors' own research on the basis of Swiss Re (2011, 2017, 2020, 2021).

life insurance markets. Their combined share in the European life insurance market was 67.7% in 2020. The biggest four European non-life insurance markets operate in Germany, the United Kingdom, France and the Netherlands. Their combined share in the European non-life insurance market was 64.2% in 2020. All in all (life and non-life insurance combined), the four largest European insurance markets are present in the United Kingdom, Germany, France and Italy. Their combined share in the European life insurance market was 64.3% in 2020.

According to a Swiss Re study (2021), the biggest insurance markets worldwide exist in the United States, China and Japan. Details of the biggest insurance markets globally, measured with premium, are set out in Table 2.5. The figures concern 1980, 2020 and 2030 forecasts.

The changes in the structure of the global insurance market in the years examined are also depicted in Figure 2.3.

An analysis of Table 2.5 and Figure 2.3 demonstrates that the four European markets are among the top ten global insurance markets. Their significance in the world market clearly declines, especially in the 2030 forecast, which projects a considerable expansion in the share of the Chinese market. The falling importance and share in the global insurance market are particularly true of Germany (in 1980 – 8.0%, in 2020 – 4.1%), as well as the United Kingdom (in 1980 – 6.9%, in 2020 – 5.4%) and France (in 1980 – 5.1%, in 2020 – 3.7%). Only the Italian insurance market has experienced a growing share in the global market (in 1980 – 1.7%, in 2020 – 2.6%).

Development of insurance markets in the EU

The sizes and development standards of insurance markets in the EU countries are varied. This arises from the size of a country, its population and level of economic development. The date of joining the EU also seems to be a major determinant of an insurance market development – those in the old EU countries are better developed than in the new EU states.

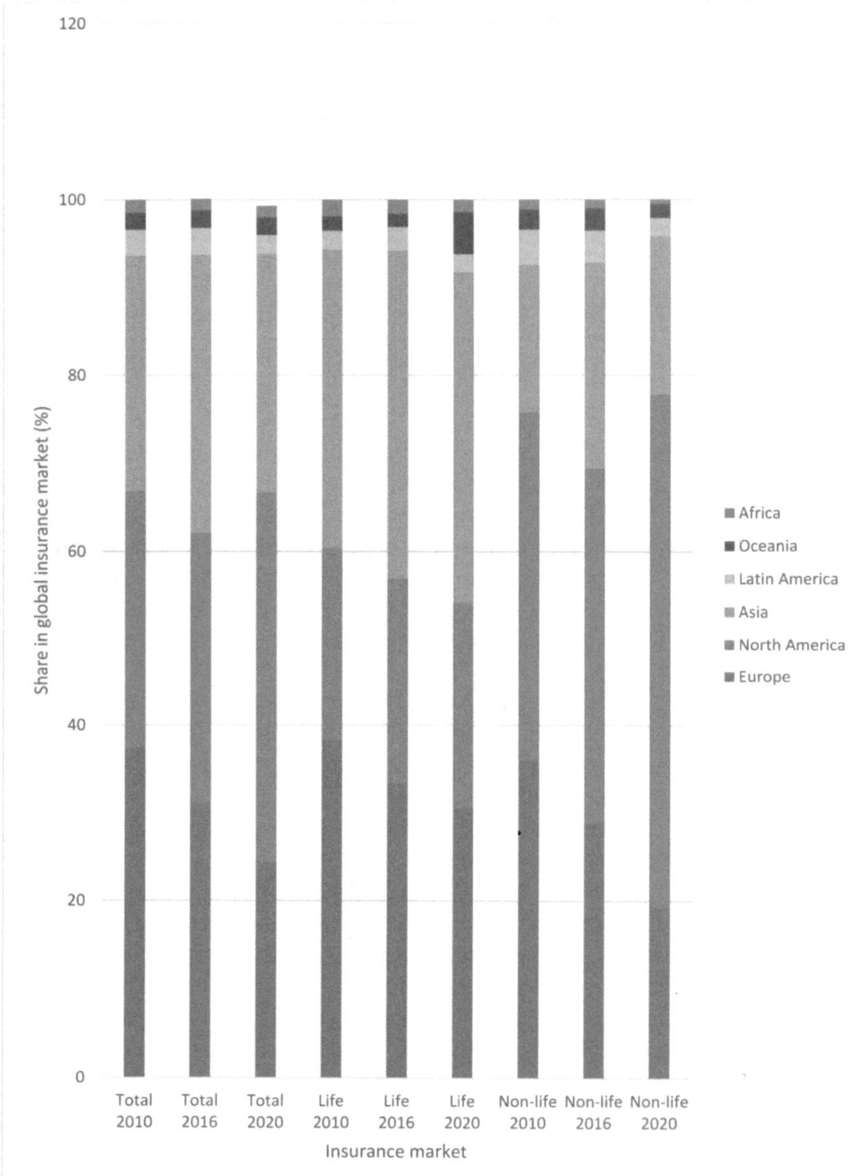

Figure 2.1 The shares in the world insurance market by regions in 2010–2020 (%).

Table 2.3 The European insurance market in 2010–2020 (gross written premium, dollar, million)

	Total			*Life insurance*			*Non-life insurance*		
Specification	*2010*	*2016*	*2020*	*2010*	*2016*	*2020*	*2010*	*2016*	*2020*
United Kingdom	119,972	304,208	338,320	213,831	199,369	238,890	96,141	104,839	99,430
France	280,082	237,643	231,347	192,428	152,817	136,611	87,654	84,826	94,736
Italy	173,348	162,383	161,973	122,063	122,438	118,612	51,285	39,945	43,361
Germany	239,817	215,021	258,566	114,868	94,661	106,571	124,949	120,360	151,995
Spain	80,704	68,599	66,322	39,296	34,459	24,926	41,408	34,140	41,396
Netherlands	106,628	80,131	87,529	34,674	16,385	13,920	71,954	63,746	73,609
Ireland	47,902	59,295	58,089	39,296	51,233	50,654	8606	8062	7435
Switzerland	52,119	61,678	62,669	28,809	31,151	31,810	23,310	27,219	30,859
Other Countries	519,865	281,063	275,851	180,396	154,094	164,886	149,468	128,277	110,965
Total	1,620,437	1,470,021	1,540,666	965,661	856,607	886,880	654,775	611,414	653,786

Source: The authors' own research on the basis of Swiss Re (2011, 2017, 2020, 2021).

Table 2.4 The structure of the European insurance market in 2010–2020 (%)

	Total			*Life insurance*			*Non-life insurance*		
Specification	*2010*	*2016*	*2020*	*2010*	*2016*	*2020*	*2010*	*2016*	*2020*
United Kingdom	7.4	20.7	22.0	22.1	23.2	26.9	14.7	17.1	15.2
France	17.3	16.2	15.0	19.9	17.8	15.4	13.4	13.9	14.5
Italy	10.7	11.0	10.5	12.6	14.3	13.4	7.8	6.5	6.6
Germany	14.8	14.6	16.8	11.9	11.0	12.0	19.1	19.7	23.2
Spain	5.0	4.7	4.3	4.1	4.1	2.8	6.3	5.6	6.3
Netherlands	6.6	5.5	5.7	3.6	1.9	1.6	11.0	10.4	11.3
Ireland	2.9	4.0	3.8	4.1	6.1	5.7	1.3	1.3	1.1
Switzerland	3.2	4.2	4.1	3.0	3.6	3.6	3.6	4.5	4.7
Other Countries	32.1	19.1	17.8	18.7	18.0	18.6	22.8	21.0	17.1
Total	100.0	100.0	100.0	100.0	100.0	100.0	100.0	100.0	100.0

Source: The authors' own research on the basis of Swiss Re (2011, 2017, 2020, 2021).

The development of the EU countries' insurance markets is analysed by means of the following measures:

- The number of insurance companies.
- The share of life assurance in the insurance market (life gross written premium/total gross written premium).
- Penetration rate (gross written premium/Gross Domestic Product (GDP)).
- Density rate (gross written premium/population).

The insurance markets of all the EU countries are studied regardless of the date of joining or leaving the EU – 28 countries. The years 1999–2019 are covered. Annual financial data from the following databases are utilised: EIOPA Database (2021), Eurostat Database (2021), OECD Statistics (2021) and Insurance Europe (2021).

The number of insurance companies in EU countries

The number of insurance companies in the particular EU countries varies. In general, this is related to population in a given country, the level of its economic development and the development of insurance market. The number of insurance companies in the particular EU countries in 1999–2019 is shown in Table 2.6 and Figure 2.4.

An analysis of the data in Figure 2.4 shows clear differences between the number of insurance companies in the EU-15 and the remaining EU countries. There are more than 100 in all the EU-15 countries with the exception of Austria and Portugal. In the remaining EU countries, the number of insurers is below 100. The EU-15 countries are also more varied in respect of the number of insurance companies. There are both those where there are fewer than 100 (Austria and Portugal) and those with

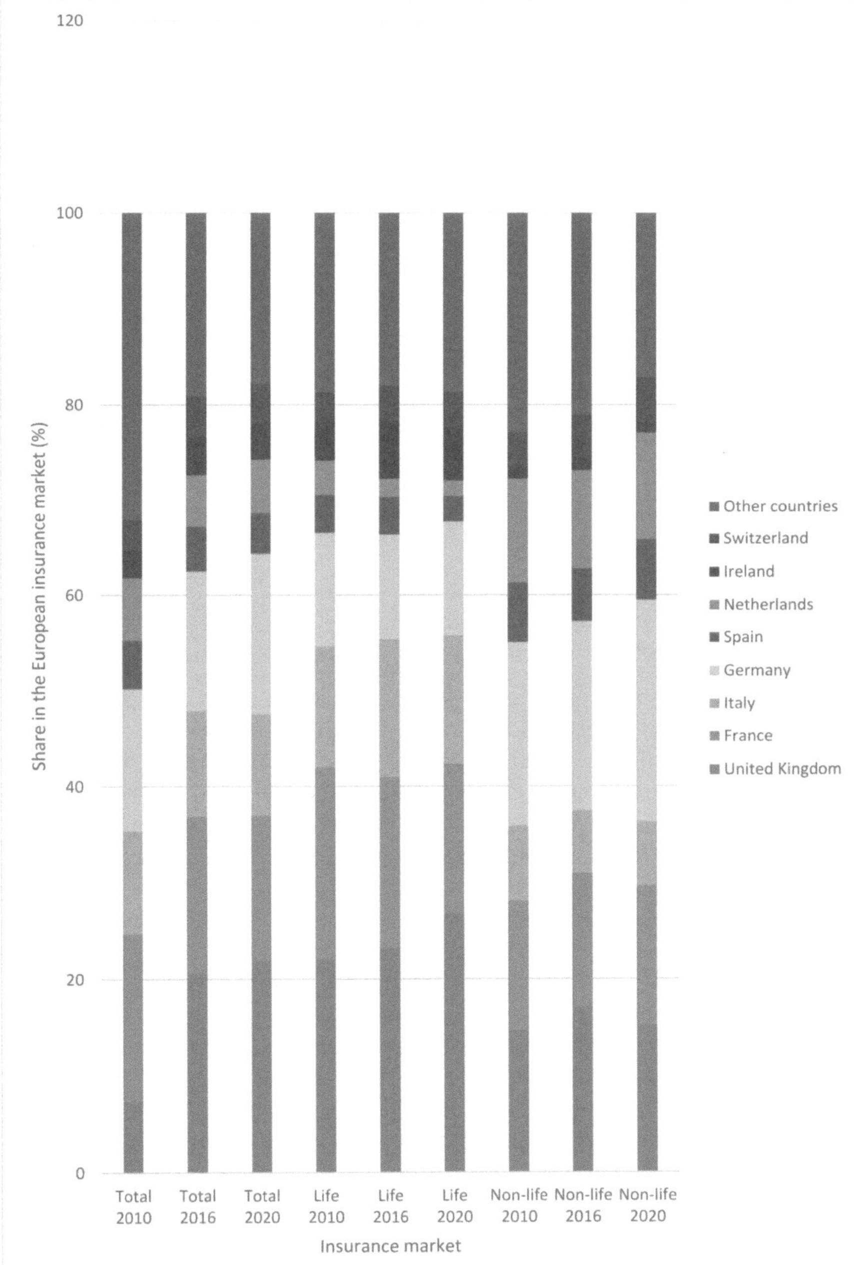

Figure 2.2 The structure of the European insurance market in 2010–2020 (%).

Table 2.5 Top ten insurance markets by total direct premium volume in 1980–2030F

	Total premium volume (Dollar, bn)			*Global market share (%)*		
Specification	*1980*	*2020*	*2030F*	*1980*	*2020*	*2030F*
United States	229	2530	3660	46.0	40.3	36.0
China	-	655	1777	0.0	10.4	18.0
Japan	75	414	621	15.0	6.6	6.1
United Kingdom	35	338	404	6.9	5.4	4.0
Germany	40	258	320	8.0	4.1	3.2
France	26	231	325	5.1	3.7	3.2
South Korea	2	193	258	0.3	3.1	2.5
Italy	8	161	247	1.7	2.6	2.4
Canada	13	143	205	2.6	2.3	2.0
Taiwan	1	113	205	0.1	1.8	2.0

Source: The authors' own research on the basis of Swiss Re (2021).

more than 300 insurers (France, Germany, Luxembourg, the Netherlands, Spain and the United Kingdom).

The share of life insurance in the insurance market in EU countries

The structure of an insurance market is measured with the share of life insurance in the total insurance market. It is hypothesised that the larger the share of life insurance, the more positive the impact on the development of an insurance market. Studies in this field have been conducted by, among others, Haiss and Sümegi (2008, pp. 405–431) and Arena (2008, pp. 921–946).

The evolution of the share of life insurance in the EU insurance market in 1999–2019 is illustrated in Table 2.7 and Figure 2.5.

An analysis of the life insurance's shares in the insurance markets helps to divide the EU insurance markets examined into two main groupings:

- The EU-15 countries, where the share is generally 50% or more. It is maximum in Luxembourg, around 90%, and Ireland, approximately 80%.
- The new EU member states, where the share of life assurance in the insurance market is about 30%. It is the lowest in Bulgaria, Slovenia and Romania – below 20%. The situation is somewhat better in the markets of Latvia, where the share of life insurance in the market has been growing but is still below 30%, and Croatia, where it has been varied in the period studied, ranging from 16.5% to 32.4%.

The penetration rate of the insurance market in EU countries

The penetration rate, the relation of gross written premium to GDP, is treated as a key ratio characterising the development of an insurance

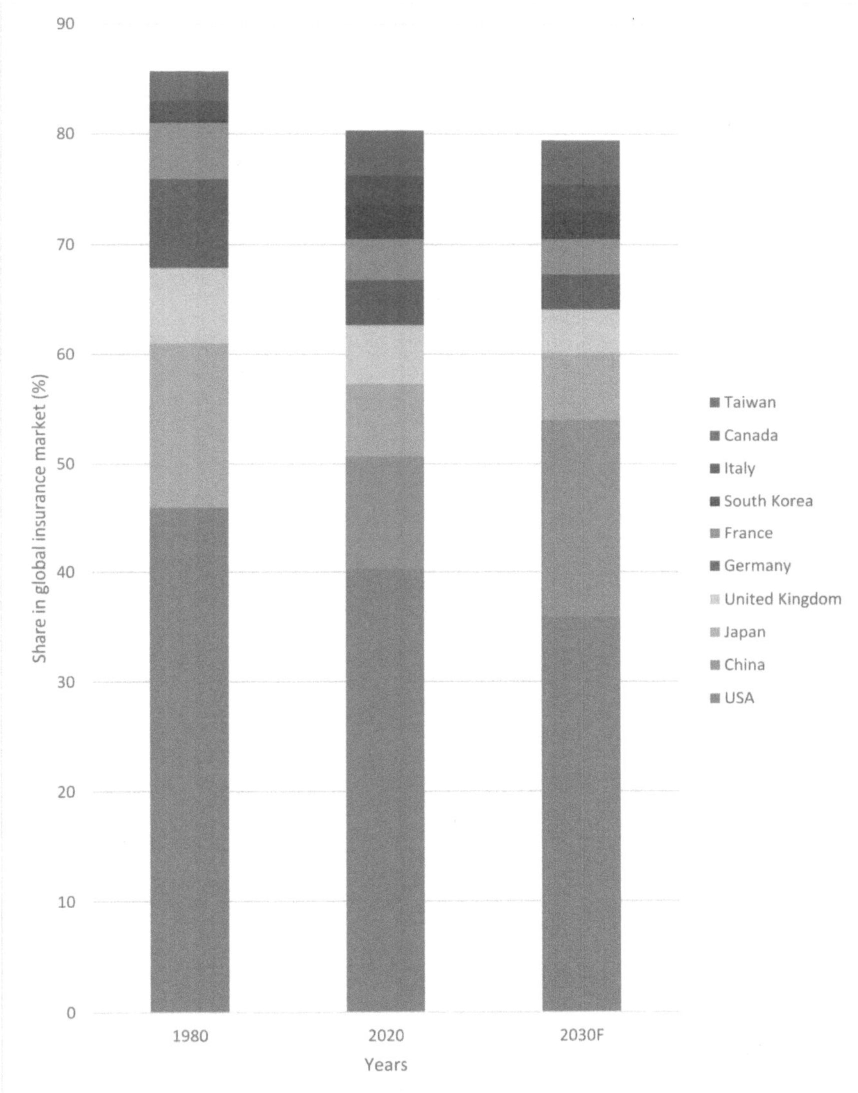

Figure 2.3 Top ten insurance markets in 1980–2030F (%).

market. This is upheld by the research of Browne and Kim (1993), Beck and Webb (2003), Zhang and Zhu (2005), Pye (2005), Ducháčková and Daňhel (2006, 2010), Li *et al.* (2007), Chui and Kwok (2008), Han *et al.* (2010), Zheng *et al.* (2009), Cristian (2010), Sankaramuthukumar and Alamelu (2012), Medveď and Kavčič (2012), Bednarczyk (2012), Brokešová and Vachálková (2016), Kurylo *et al.* (2017), Burić *et al.* (2017), Bukowski and Lament (2019, 2020), inter alia.

Table 2.6 Number of insurance companies in EU countries in 1999–2019

EU countries	1999	2000	2001	2002	2003	2004	2005	2006	2007	2008	2009	2010	2011	2012	2013	2014	2015	2016	2017	2018	2019
AT	59	58	67	55	54	54	54	54	52	52	52	52	52	48	47	44	42	39	38	36	36
BE	139	134	131	125	120	117	171	162	156	151	148	149	151	136	130	128	123	118	114	115	113
BG[1]	40	40	37	37	37	37	37	37	36	35	34	33	35	35	36	44	46	42	38	36	35
HR[2]	24	24	24	24	24	24	25	20	23	25	27	26	26	27	26	25	23	21	20	18	16
CY[3]	30	30	30	30	28	28	28	28	28	29	29	29	29	29	34	33	32	32	32	32	32
CZ[4]	42	41	43	42	42	40	45	49	52	54	53	53	54	53	52	53	55	53	49	47	46
DK	196	196	196	196	192	192	189	182	179	174	202	202	196	176	172	157	153	155	156	160	147
EE[5]	13	13	13	13	13	13	13	13	13	13	12	13	12	17	17	17	16	17	16	18	18
FI	171	168	162	159	152	136	131	128	120	118	117	92	91	55	55	51	51	48	47	68	67
FR	459	462	466	456	444	423	415	415	387	369	386	381	371	339	329	318	301	647	631	615	598
DE	683	666	650	750	746	740	727	510	510	511	485	492	489	464	385	379	375	369	368	367	370
GR	120	117	113	105	105	105	105	102	80	73	75	58	55	55	52	48	48	45	42	39	38
HU[6]	57	61	63	67	68	65	42	40	42	47	49	51	50	50	47	47	45	43	40	37	34
IE	209	175	184	184	224	217	226	227	231	255	255	242	322	289	269	266	259	238	251	251	245
IT	250	252	256	251	249	246	245	247	243	247	241	242	239	235	233	222	220	214	213	218	214
LV[7]	19	19	18	18	18	18	20	20	16	16	25	24	22	22	19	21	22	19	17	17	18
LI[8]	27	27	27	27	26	26	26	28	28	28	28	28	25	25	24	24	24	21	21	20	20
LU	351	357	357	361	365	368	357	357	356	353	344	343	331	327	317	317	307	297	291	291	288
MT[9]	45	45	45	45	45	45	45	45	45	45	45	50	54	58	60	62	61	61	63	61	61
NL	375	375	371	357	339	324	309	315	299	289	282	261	247	220	268	186	186	147	140	131	131
PL[10]	63	69	72	74	78	72	71	75	70	68	66	63	64	59	58	57	61	61	61	60	59
PT	94	87	86	81	74	70	70	75	84	83	86	83	78	78	77	77	79	73	73	78	70
RO[11]	38	38	39	39	39	39	40	41	42	43	45	43	43	40	38	37	35	31	31	29	28
SK[12]	28	29	28	29	28	26	26	24	34	35	34	36	38	38	38	38	38	38	38	38	38
SI[13]	20	20	20	20	20	20	20	20	21	21	20	20	21	22	22	22	23	22	21	22	22
ES	321	310	299	296	353	332	313	298	291	295	296	287	280	270	265	255	241	231	220	211	204
SE	194	194	184	184	172	192	207	195	210	236	245	240	217	209	207	204	207	194	203	175	176
GB[14]	712	724	777	777	544	544	535	512	507	510	519	503	499	490	476	466	454	294	294	272	294

Years: 1999–2019

Source: The authors' own research on the basis of EIOPA Database (2021), Eurostat Database (2021), OECD Statistics (2021) and Insurance Europe (2021).

Explanation: AT – Austria, BE – Belgium, BG – Bulgaria, HR – Croatia, CY – Cyprus, CZ – Czech Republic, DK – Denmark, EE – Estonia, FI – Finland, FR – France, DE – Germany, GR – Greece, HU – Hungary, IE – Ireland, IT – Italy, LV – Latvia, LI – Lithuania, LU – Luxembourg, MT – Malta, NL – Netherlands, PL – Poland, PT – Portugal, RO – Romania, SK – Slovak Republic, SI – Slovenia, ES – Spain, SE – Sweden, GB – United Kingdom.

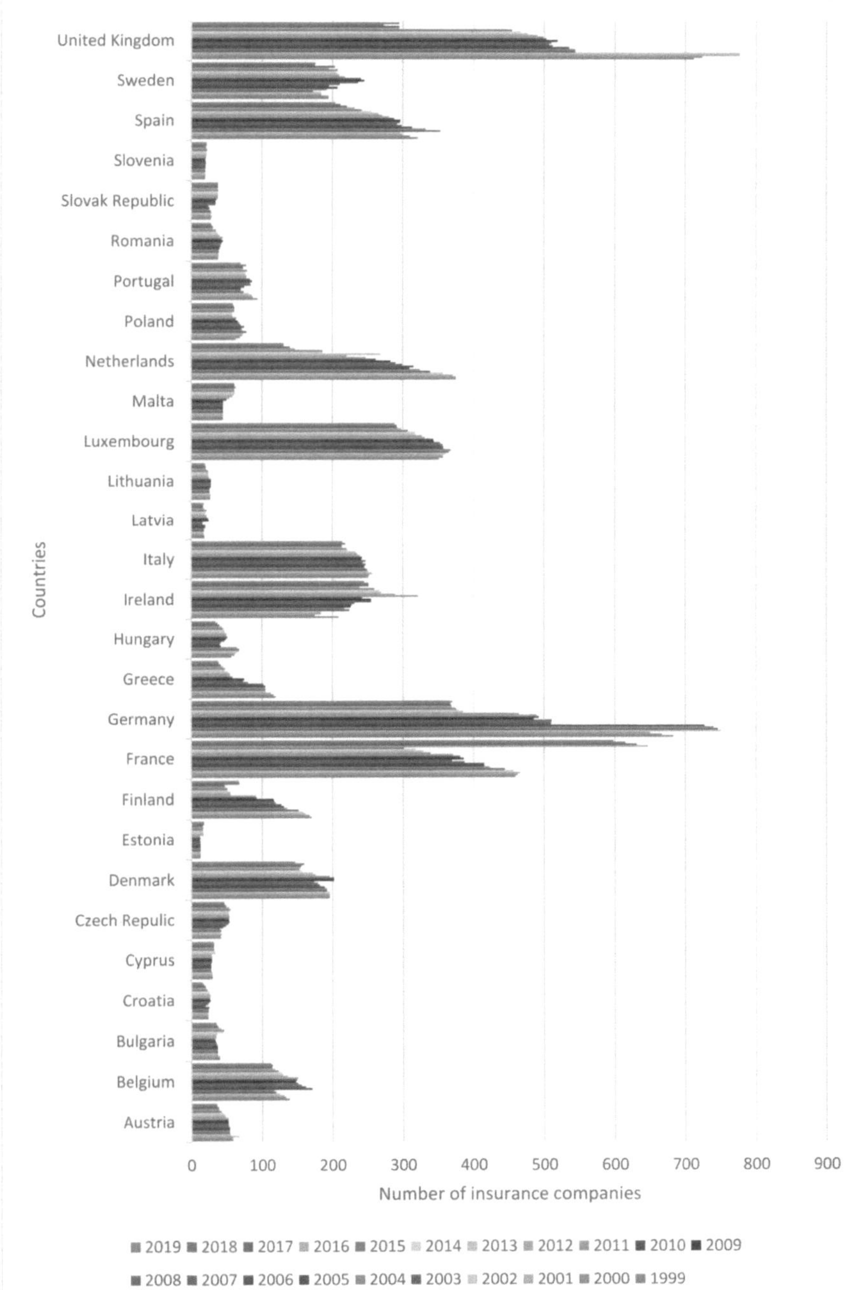

Figure 2.4 Number of insurance companies in the EU countries in 1999–2019.

Table 2.7 Share of life insurance in insurance market in EU countries in 1999–2019 (%)

EU countries	*Years*																				
	1999	*2000*	*2001*	*2002*	*2003*	*2004*	*2005*	*2006*	*2007*	*2008*	*2009*	*2010*	*2011*	*2012*	*2013*	*2014*	*2015*	*2016*	*2017*	*2018*	*2019*
AT	38.8	40.5	42.9	38.8	36.9	39.3	40.8	41.7	40.8	40.2	39.6	38.5	37.9	35.5	34.1	35.4	35.2	32.4	31.6	29.9	29.9
BE	58.5	64.2	64.2	62.0	68.0	70.0	75.5	70.1	70.5	66.6	64.8	65.0	63.1	64.7	57.7	56.4	55.4	54.4	53.6	54.7	51.7
BG[15]	14.2	14.8	14.9	14.8	14.9	15.4	15.7	15.8	16.1	16.4	16.5	16.7	16.8	16.7	17.6	19.1	19.9	20.8	15.8	14.0	12.7
HR[16]	16.5	16.8	18.2	20.7	22.3	23.7	25.8	26.5	27.4	26.3	26.5	26.6	27.2	27.2	28.0	30.8	33.6	33.3	32.4	31.8	29.1
CY[17]	65.3	67.2	55.1	53.4	50.2	43.0	53.5	46.0	46.0	44.9	44.2	44.9	45.0	43.0	41.9	41.5	42.0	42.9	43.5	44.0	42.8
CZ[18]	31.5	32.2	35.0	37.5	38.8	39.2	38.3	38.6	40.7	40.6	41.7	45.9	46.4	46.9	45.7	45.0	41.1	40.5	38.2	36.6	32.0
DK	58.7	60.6	61.8	57.4	58.7	58.4	64.8	66.1	65.4	67.5	67.4	67.9	68.1	68.6	65.3	67.7	68.9	68.6	69.0	69.9	71.3
EE[19]	35.7	36.3	38.6	38.2	38.2	39.1	39.5	40.8	40.7	40.8	40.5	40.5	39.7	33.8	29.3	30.3	31.1	30.0	27.2	25.1	25.7
FI	56.7	62.7	55.4	54.2	50.0	48.9	49.4	47.2	45.9	45.2	49.1	59.5	51.1	51.1	56.8	57.4	58.2	50.5	50.7	50.6	51.8
FR	63.0	66.2	63.2	61.2	62.5	64.4	66.7	61.6	59.7	64.3	66.8	67.1	63.8	62.1	62.4	64.1	64.1	58.0	55.2	55.2	55.7
DE	40.3	40.4	40.2	38.5	39.7	36.6	37.9	41.9	41.8	42.0	46.1	47.8	45.6	35.4	36.0	35.9	33.9	33.1	32.0	31.8	32.7
GR	54.9	51.5	49.2	45.7	44.3	47.5	49.0	47.9	48.4	47.1	45.9	43.2	43.7	43.1	41.3	49.4	50.4	47.2	50.4	49.4	50.9
HU[20]	41.1	45.8	41.7	41.0	40.0	40.6	43.9	50.4	54.8	52.4	50.3	53.1	54.5	53.0	54.4	54.8	51.1	49.5	48.2	46.2	44.2
IE	69.9	74.4	69.0	68.4	66.3	72.5	76.3	80.1	83.5	79.6	80.9	80.2	79.2	80.2	80.6	82.2	79.6	68.5	79.5	75.3	71.9
IT	56.5	57.9	59.7	61.7	63.6	63.6	66.2	65.3	61.8	59.1	68.9	71.7	67.0	66.4	71.4	76.8	77.8	75.8	74.9	74.6	75.1
LV[21]	15.9	15.8	15.8	15.6	15.4	15.8	16.1	15.9	16.3	15.7	15.8	22.9	18.4	17.5	18.9	20.6	21.6	23.2	22.4	19.2	26.6
LI[22]	30.6	30.7	30.8	31.3	31.5	31.7	32.4	32.7	33.8	33.9	34.2	34.7	32.9	31.9	31.9	35.7	36.5	34.7	29.1	28.2	28.5
LU	87.0	87.0	85.5	84.9	89.8	90.6	90.8	91.3	89.3	89.8	93.2	94.2	90.3	93.3	91.9	93.8	92.3	91.5	91.7	91.7	90.6
MT[23]	35.6	35.6	36.3	36.5	36.5	37.5	38.1	38.2	38.5	38.2	38.0	32.0	46.1	42.0	41.3	40.6	33.0	33.3	37.9	38.9	40.2
NL	57.6	57.1	58.4	54.4	53.1	51.6	51.1	56.1	56.0	54.5	50.8	51.0	51.4	47.5	47.4	47.7	43.6	49.6	48.2	46.2	46.8
PL[24]	31.8	33.5	34.4	35.0	37.3	37.8	49.4	56.2	58.3	65.6	58.9	58.0	55.7	58.0	54.0	52.1	50.2	42.5	39.4	34.9	32.3
PT	56.2	55.4	53.6	52.8	55.8	58.8	67.4	66.5	67.3	71.0	70.7	74.6	64.2	63.2	70.4	72.9	67.4	59.6	58.5	61.7	56.7
RO[25]	15.2	15.6	16.7	17.0	17.1	17.9	18.5	18.9	18.9	19.2	19.4	19.7	20.2	20.7	22.0	19.2	19.9	18.9	20.2	20.6	20.6
SK[26]	33.1	40.7	42.9	43.0	40.8	40.2	45.6	47.2	49.6	52.3	51.4	53.0	53.1	53.8	55.4	54.2	51.2	69.5	73.5	50.3	48.5
SI[27]	20.1	20.4	20.8	20.8	20.9	21.3	21.5	21.6	21.7	29.3	21.9	22.3	22.0	22.1	22.3	22.8	23.1	22.5	22.4	21.6	20.8
ES	51.7	56.7	53.2	53.5	41.9	41.4	41.4	44.1	40.7	44.0	47.6	47.5	46.9	46.4	44.5	43.8	43.5	47.1	44.8	43.6	41.5
SE	59.5	59.3	58.0	58.5	54.1	53.9	57.8	55.5	49.7	46.6	50.7	48.8	49.6	53.9	52.1	69.6	73.3	74.9	76.0	75.6	75.5
GB[28]	68.8	72.3	66.1	63.0	58.9	61.7	64.3	79.5	83.1	76.2	75.9	73.6	73.4	75.4	72.4	73.3	73.2	68.7	68.3	71.6	7.9

Source: The authors' own research on the basis of EIOPA Database (2021), Eurostat Database (2021), OECD Statistics (2021) and Insurance Europe (2021).

Explanation: AT – Austria, BE – Belgium, BG – Bulgaria, HR – Croatia, CY – Cyprus, CZ – Czech Republic, DK – Denmark, EE – Estonia, FI – Finland, FR – France, DE – Germany, GR – Greece, HU – Hungary, IE – Ireland, IT – Italy, LV – Latvia, LI – Lithuania, LU – Luxembourg, MT – Malta, NL – Netherlands, PL – Poland, PT – Portugal, RO – Romania, SK – Slovak Republic, SI – Slovenia, ES – Spain, SE – Sweden, GB – United Kingdom.

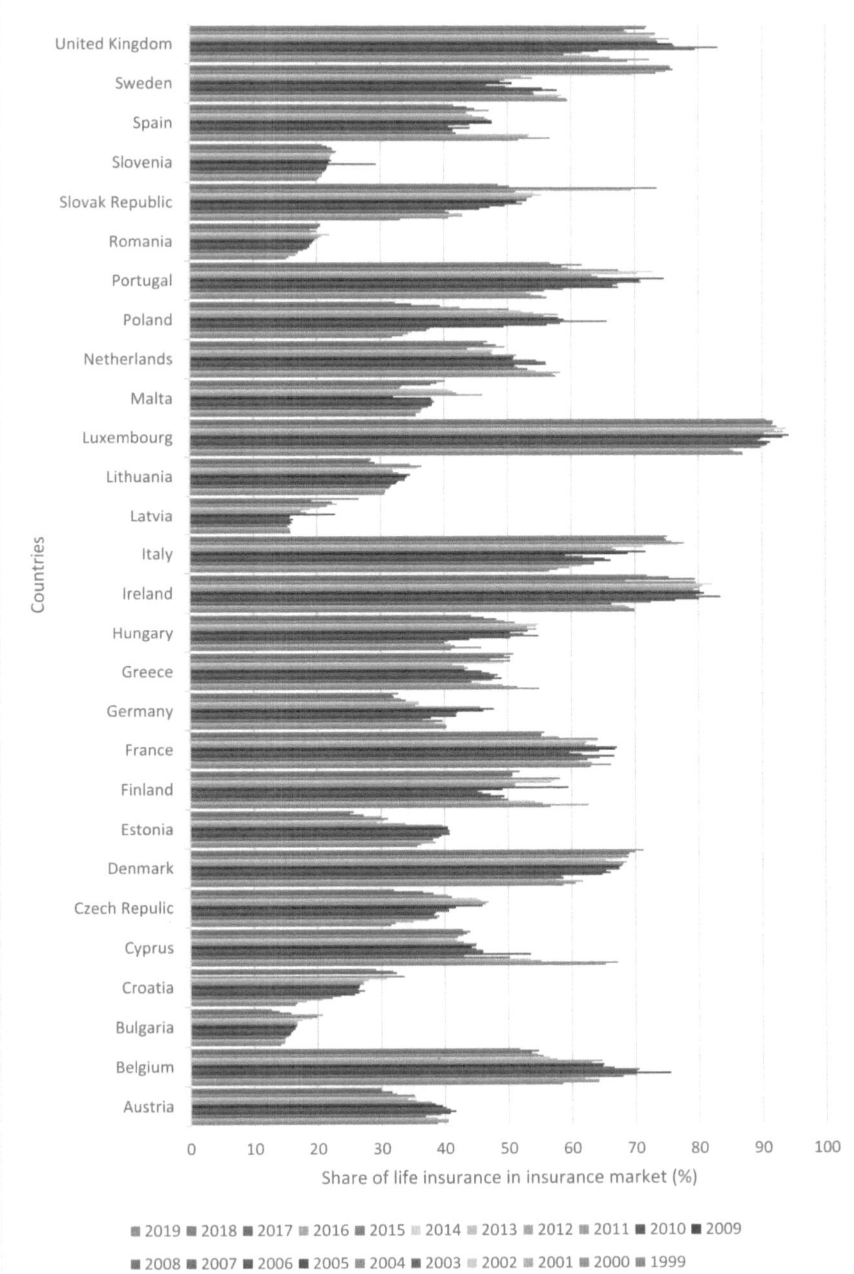

Figure 2.5 Share of life insurance in insurance market in the EU countries in 1999–2019 (%).

The penetration rate represents changes in the relative significance of the insurance sector in a national economy. The rate's sensitivity to GDP variations is a weakness. If GDP changes a lot in a given year, the penetration rate may be highly variable even if the situation in an insurance market remains basically stable at the same time (Brokešová and Vachálková, 2016).

The evolution of the penetration rate in the EU countries in 1999–2019 is depicted in Table 2.8 and Figure 2.6.

The data concerning the penetration rate indicate that the insurance sector is most important in countries like Luxembourg, Ireland and the United Kingdom. There are some groups of countries with similar levels of the rate, proof of the comparable levels of development of both the countries themselves and their insurance markets. This is true of the following groups:

- The EU-15 – the penetration rate is in the range of 2–40%. It's a highly mixed grouping, largely due to its numbers. It includes countries of very high GNPs and a concomitant major importance of the insurance sector in their economies (e.g., Luxembourg) and countries with very well-developed insurance sectors and their relatively lesser, though still high, significance to economies (e.g., France and Germany).
- The Visegrad Group (Poland, Czech Republic, Slovak Republic and Hungary) – the penetration rate is in the range of 2–3%. Both the economic development and the development of insurance industries in these countries are similar.
- Scandinavian countries (Sweden, Finland and Denmark) – the penetration rate is in the range of 2.5–10.8%. The rate has varied in the period reviewed, a sign of the changing importance of insurance in their economies. The penetration rate has been at its steadiest in Denmark.
- The new EU member states (Bulgaria, Croatia, Cyprus, Czech Republic, Estonia, Hungary, Latvia, Lithuania, Malta, Poland, Romania, Slovenia and Slovak Republic) – the penetration rate is in the range of 0.7–15.4%. A highly diverse group, largely due to the differing levels of economic development. The date of joining the EU appears a major factor ordering the group – the penetration rate is better in those that joined the EU earlier. Two unique countries (Cyprus and Malta) should be distinguished here, whose penetration rate is clearly greater than in the remaining countries, a result of the far higher significance of their insurance sectors in their economies than in the other countries included in this group.

The density rate of the insurance market in EU countries

The rate of insurance density denotes the relation of gross written premium to population and reflects population of a given country, a major determinant of demand for insurance products. Thus, it represents a real growth of insurance. This rate is essential to comparisons of insurance development between countries. Like in the case of penetration rate, this is corroborated

Table 2.8 Penetration rate of insurance market in EU countries in 1999–2019 (%)

EU countries	Years																				
	1999	2000	2001	2002	2003	2004	2005	2006	2007	2008	2009	2010	2011	2012	2013	2014	2015	2016	2017	2018	2019
AT	5.4	5.4	5.6	5.5	5.6	5.6	5.4	5.3	5.0	5.4	5.6	5.6	5.3	5.1	5.1	5.1	5.0	4.7	4.5	4.4	4.4
BE	6.9	7.5	7.6	8.0	8.9	9.4	10.7	8.9	9.0	8.1	8.0	7.9	7.5	8.2	6.9	6.9	6.4	6.2	5.9	6.0	6.1
BG[29]	1.5	1.5	1.6	1.6	1.6	1.7	1.8	2.1	2.2	2.2	2.1	2.0	1.8	1.7	2.1	2.1	2.1	2.1	2.1	2.2	2.2
HR[30]	2.3	2.3	2.4	2.4	2.5	2.6	2.7	2.7	2.7	2.7	2.8	2.7	2.7	2.7	2.7	2.6	2.6	2.5	2.4	2.5	2.6
CY[31]	9.2	9.2	9.3	9.8	9.2	9.0	8.9	8.9	9.1	4.0	4.3	4.3	4.3	4.3	4.2	4.2	4.3	4.2	4.4	4.3	3.9
CZ[32]	3.0	2.9	3.1	3.3	3.7	3.6	3.5	3.4	3.4	3.4	3.6	3.8	3.7	3.6	3.7	3.5	3.2	2.9	2.8	2.7	2.8
DK	6.3	6.1	6.6	7.5	6.7	6.8	7.8	8.2	8.8	9.1	9.1	9.3	9.8	9.9	9.9	10.4	10.4	10.3	11.0	11.1	10.8
EE[33]	1.5	1.5	1.6	1.7	1.8	2.0	2.2	1.7	1.0	1.3	1.7	2.8	2.3	2.6	3.0	3.1	3.3	3.3	3.4	3.5	3.5
FI	4.3	4.8	4.0	3.9	3.6	3.5	3.7	3.5	3.1	3.1	3.6	4.5	3.6	3.5	4.7	5.0	5.0	4.0	3.8	1.8	2.5
FR	8.3	8.7	8.2	8.2	8.6	9.2	9.8	12.1	11.0	9.1	10.2	10.2	9.2	8.6	8.8	9.2	9.3	10.7	10.7	10.6	10.6
DE	6.5	6.4	6.3	6.6	6.9	6.9	7.1	6.7	6.5	6.4	6.4	6.4	6.1	6.5	6.7	6.5	6.3	6.1	6.3	6.3	6.6
GR	2.0	1.8	1.7	1.7	1.8	1.8	1.8	2.1	2.2	2.1	2.2	2.2	2.3	2.3	2.3	2.1	1.9	1.9	2.0	2.0	2.1
HU[34]	2.5	2.8	2.7	2.8	2.9	2.8	3.0	3.3	3.6	3.2	3.1	3.0	2.8	2.6	2.6	2.5	2.3	2.4	2.4	2.3	2.4
IE	14.0	20.1	13.4	13.6	14.8	16.8	18.0	19.5	23.0	18.9	19.5	20.1	18.4	19.8	18.6	19.9	16.4	17.6	14.6	12.1	12.0
IT	5.5	5.5	5.9	6.5	7.0	7.0	7.5	7.1	6.4	5.8	7.4	7.7	6.6	6.4	7.3	8.7	8.8	7.9	7.5	7.6	7.8
LV[35]	1.4	1.5	1.5	1.5	1.5	1.5	1.6	1.6	1.8	1.8	1.9	1.8	1.9	2.0	2.0	2.1	2.1	2.1	2.4	2.6	2.8
LI[36]	1.4	1.4	1.5	1.5	1.5	1.5	1.5	1.5	1.5	1.5	1.5	1.6	1.5	1.5	1.6	1.6	1.7	1.8	1.8	1.9	1.9
LU	27.5	27.2	25.6	24.3	25.3	28.7	33.7	34.5	30.1	28.4	44.8	51.2	31.3	43.8	39.6	43.2	36.5	33.2	37.7	34.5	37.3
MT[37]	8.5	8.3	8.9	9.0	9.5	9.9	10.1	13.3	15.4	5.4	6.0	6.4	6.8	6.3	4.6	4.5	4.8	5.0	5.0	4.9	4.4
NL	9.2	8.9	9.0	8.6	8.9	9.1	8.7	7.8	7.6	7.4	7.1	5.7	6.4	6.0	5.7	5.3	4.8	9.8	9.4	9.3	9.2
PL[38]	2.7	2.7	2.8	2.7	2.9	2.9	3.0	3.4	3.6	4.5	3.7	3.7	3.6	3.8	3.4	3.1	2.9	2.9	3.0	2.8	2.6
PT	5.5	6.0	5.6	5.8	6.3	6.6	8.3	7.6	7.6	8.3	7.8	8.6	6.1	6.0	7.2	7.8	6.7	5.5	5.5	5.8	5.3
RO[39]	0.7	0.7	0.7	0.8	0.8	0.8	0.8	0.9	1.1	1.2	1.2	1.3	1.2	0.9	0.9	1.1	0.9	1.2	1.1	1.1	1.1
SK[40]	1.9	2.0	2.1	2.2	2.3	2.5	2.5	2.5	2.6	2.9	3.2	3.1	2.9	2.9	2.9	2.9	2.6	2.5	5.2	2.7	2.6
SI[41]	4.0	4.4	4.8	5.0	5.1	5.2	5.3	5.4	5.4	5.3	5.2	5.2	5.1	5.3	5.1	4.9	4.8	4.7	4.7	4.6	4.8
ES	5.4	6.3	5.9	6.4	5.2	5.2	5.2	5.2	5.0	5.3	5.6	5.2	5.4	5.3	5.2	5.1	5.0	5.4	5.2	5.1	4.8
SE	6.7	7.7	7.7	7.8	7.0	7.3	7.5	6.8	5.9	5.6	5.3	4.7	4.5	4.1	4.3	8.2	7.7	7.3	7.9	8.5	8.5
GB[42]	13.9	14.7	13.2	13.1	13.5	13.5	13.1	18.3	19.7	14.7	13.4	12.3	11.7	12.5	11.0	10.7	10.2	9.6	12.6	13.1	11.9

Source: The authors' own research on the basis of EIOPA Database (2021), Eurostat Database (2021), OECD Statistics (2021) and Insurance Europe (2021).

Explanation: AT – Austria, BE – Belgium, BG – Bulgaria, HR – Croatia, CY – Cyprus, CZ – Czech Republic, DK – Denmark, EE – Estonia, FI – Finland, FR – France, DE – Germany, GR – Greece, HU – Hungary, IE – Ireland, IT – Italy, LV – Latvia, LI – Lithuania, LU – Luxembourg, MT – Malta, NL – Netherlands, PL – Poland, PT – Portugal, RO – Romania, SK –, Slovak Republic, SI – Slovenia, ES – Spain, SE – Sweden, GB – United Kingdom.

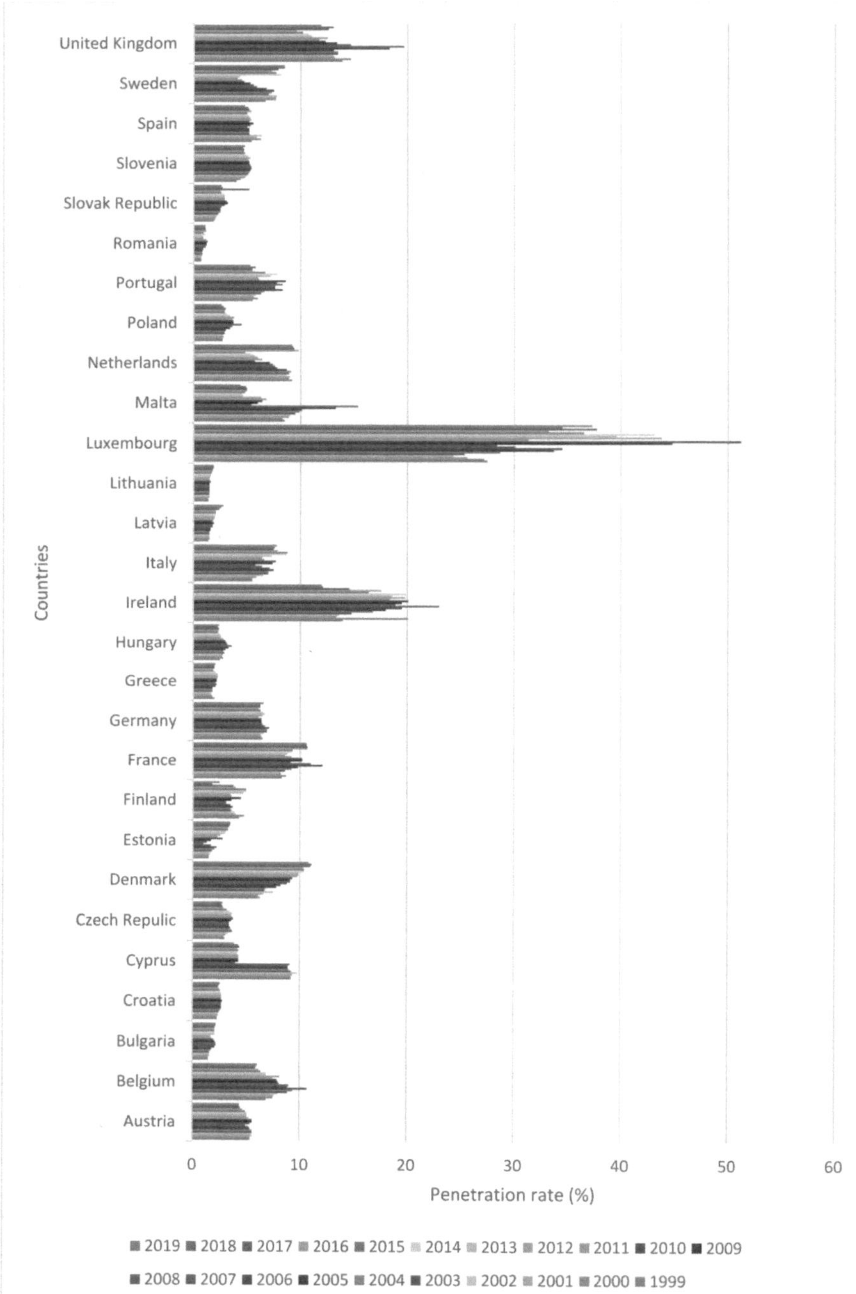

Figure 2.6 Penetration rate of insurance market in the EU countries in 1999–2019 (%).

by, among others, Browne and Kim (1993), Beck and Webb (2003), Zhang and Zhu (2005), Pye (2005), Ducháčková and Daňhel (2006, 2010), Li *et al.* (2007), Chui and Kwok (2008), Han *et al.* (2010), Zheng *et al.* (2009), Cristian (2010), Sankaramuthukumar and Alamelu (2012), Medveď and Kavčič (2012), Bednarczyk (2012), Brokešová and Vachálková (2016), Kurylo *et al.* (2017), Burić *et al.* (2017), and Bukowski and Lament (2019, 2020).

The development of the density rate in the EU countries in 1999–2019 is presented in Table 2.9 and Figure 2.7.

An analysis of the density rate points to a great diversification in the development of insurance markets in the EU countries studied. A maximum density rate in the entire time examined was attained by Luxembourg, which, by this criterion, can be said to have a best-developed insurance market. The rate was also high in Ireland, the United Kingdom, Denmark, the Netherlands, Belgium, France and Germany. The density rate was minimum in Romania, Latvia, Lithuania and Bulgaria.

This analysis implies that the EU market is highly varied as far as the development of insurance markets measured with the density rate is concerned. The EU market is not homogenous – there are both countries noting a high economic development and a great importance of the insurance market, chiefly the EU-15, and those poorly developed with weakly developed insurance sectors, mainly the new EU member states.

The determinants of insurance market development in the EU – An econometric analysis

This study aims to identify factors determining the development of the EU countries' insurance markets in 1999–2019. The development of an insurance market is normally measured with gross written premium and its growth dynamics as well as with the density rate (gross written premium/population) and the penetration rate (gross written premium/GDP). This is affirmed by the studies of Beck and Webb (2003), Zhang and Zhu (2005), Pye (2005), Li *et al.* (2007), Han *et al.* (2010), Kurylo *et al.* (2017), Burić *et al.* (2017), inter alia.

The development of insurance markets is assumed to vary across the particular countries and depend on the following:

- Macroeconomic factors – the degree of development of an insurance market depends on the level of economic development of the country. This is corroborated by, among others, Munir and Ameer (2018), Sun *et al.* (2019) and Ostrowska-Dankiewicz and Simionescu (2020).
- The size of an insurance market measured with the number of insurance companies. The size drives the development of an insurance market, which is upheld by Outreville (1990), Ward and Zurbruegg (2002), Li *et al.* (2007), inter alia.

Table 2.9 Density rate of insurance market in EU countries in 1999–2019 (US dollar)

EU countries	Years																				
	1999	*2000*	*2001*	*2002*	*2003*	*2004*	*2005*	*2006*	*2007*	*2008*	*2009*	*2010*	*2011*	*2012*	*2013*	*2014*	*2015*	*2016*	*2017*	*2018*	*2019*
AT	1450	1335	1375	1460	1819	2052	2099	2166	2378	2847	2733	2640	2743	2491	2602	2656	2227	2142	2175	2284	2196
BE	1717	1751	1760	2010	2760	3340	3981	3464	4019	3953	3627	3513	3601	3683	3260	3308	2653	2613	2653	2903	2852
BG[43]	41	40	42	44	45	46	57	78	94	113	107	103	102	101	121	126	138	143	157	213	235
HR[44]	201	203	205	205	206	207	229	255	283	302	294	289	287	284	287	271	278	281	293	323	346
CY[45]	1467	1506	1574	1609	1689	1744	1837	1961	2124	995	1022	1030	1022	969	885	868	907	939	1032	1064	986
CZ[46]	175	177	206	270	365	426	476	526	635	787	718	769	821	732	746	711	574	554	589	650	663
DK	2080	1895	2044	2513	2744	3173	3842	4282	5191	5912	5865	5920	6069	5823	6079	6543	5609	5698	6315	6841	6485
EE[47]	101	116	124	136	140	148	186	93	148	215	257	425	422	466	587	637	581	619	701	828	835
FI	1112	1169	1006	1075	1075	1356	1466	1454	1536	1684	1750	2140	1849	1698	2370	2555	2150	1797	1802	935	1221
FR	2065	2044	1920	2073	2654	3231	3563	4583	4760	4303	4437	4314	4186	3644	3893	4110	3553	4107	4247	4568	4471
DE	1730	1542	1518	1697	2128	2408	2490	2489	2750	2979	3025	2947	3185	2889	3111	3130	2596	2602	2837	3048	3095
GR	238	217	217	250	336	410	436	537	636	693	652	618	609	511	480	457	361	358	387	413	413
HU[48]	118	130	143	189	245	292	340	384	501	509	404	402	403	336	356	359	300	316	350	380	401
IE	3595	5245	3780	5357	6083	7976	9088	10,489	14,009	11,581	10,192	9800	9574	9701	9605	11,051	10,153	11,107	10,204	9553	9492
IT	1171	1113	1216	1475	1943	2222	2421	2401	2425	2376	2757	2786	2553	2239	2600	3125	2677	2444	2436	2644	2595
LV[49]	65	68	71	75	80	81	98	130	190	209	236	203	263	276	308	343	296	299	374	461	497
LI[50]	51	55	60	64	62	60	101	162	164	142	212	192	226	222	254	272	246	273	316	369	380
LU	13,661	13,223	12,444	12,998	16,789	21,939	27,362	31,263	32,223	32,933	46,826	54,329	36,748	47,314	45,568	51,994	37,506	35,103	41,043	41,043	43,263
MT[51]	1285	1503	1678	1721	1856	2204	2204	1467	1814	687	714	790	747	641	711	828	989	1099	1168	1219	1395
NL	2424	2320	2435	2552	3194	3687	3676	3505	3950	4321	4321	2940	3495	3022	3002	2845	2176	4532	4625	4970	4871
PL[52]	118	123	141	143	165	194	247	313	409	640	427	467	502	500	475	453	372	361	420	436	418
PT	662	697	667	751	1004	1206	1566	1519	1734	2086	1821	1937	1426	1237	1569	1734	1293	1110	1189	1370	1228
RO[53]	10	13	15	15	17	20	25	37	55	76	71	72	67	63	71	85	93	100	104	109	119
SK[54]	106	110	123	150	215	276	130	336	433	558	535	519	551	507	541	543	434	556	926	638	517
SI[55]	365	405	465	476	489	514	542	592	1291	1476	1313	1240	1304	1201	1209	1197	1011	1028	1105	1222	1256
ES	842	929	916	1097	1125	1318	1392	1504	1650	1896	1808	1606	1737	1517	1529	1520	1520	1458	1470	1559	1460
SE	1933	2275	2109	2584	2630	3138	3282	3184	3169	3158	2501	2524	2780	2376	2643	4907	3960	3795	4248	4646	4574
GB[56]	3471	4107	3664	3948	4653	5240	5509	8177	9973	6981	5194	4885	4936	5315	4793	5098	4598	3949	5113	5645	5040

Source: The authors' own research on the basis of EIOPA Database (2021), Eurostat Database (2021), OECD Statistics (2021) and Insurance Europe (2021).

Explanation: AT – Austria, BE – Belgium, BG – Bulgaria, HR – Croatia, CY – Cyprus, CZ – Czech Republic, DK – Denmark, EE – Estonia, FI – Finland, FR – France, DE – Germany, GR – Greece, HU – Hungary, IE – Ireland, IT – Italy, LV – Latvia, LI – Lithuania, LU – Luxembourg, MT – Malta, NL – Netherlands, PL – Poland, PT – Portugal, RO – Romania, SK – Slovak Republic, SI – Slovenia, ES – Spain, SE – Sweden, GB – United Kingdom.

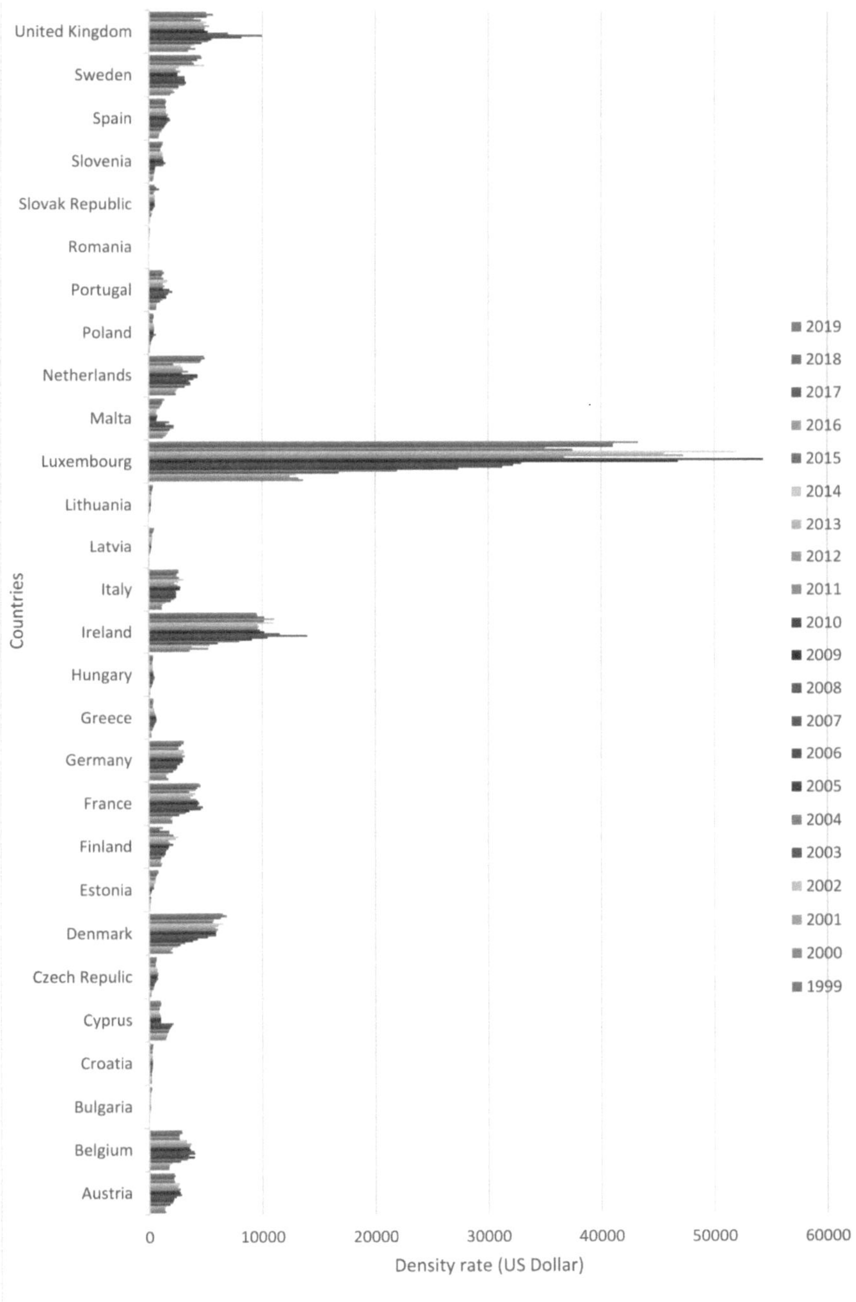

Figure 2.7 Density rate of insurance market in the EU countries in 1999–2019.

- The structure of an insurance market measured with the shares of life assurance and foreign capital in an insurance market. Research confirms a positive impact of life insurers on market development, e.g., Arena (2008), and of foreign capital on the development of an insurance market, e.g., Carson *et al.* (2014) and Bukowski and Lament (2019).
- The efficiency of an insurance market, largely dependent on financial results of its companies. This has been studied by, inter alia, Mutairi *et al.* (2021), Bukowski and Lament (2021a, 2021b) and Isik (2021).
- The significance of insurance market in the economy of a given country, measured with the density rate (gross written premium/population). The higher a density rate, the greater the development standard of an insurance market. This is upheld by T. Bednarczyk (2012) and Han *et al.* (2010), among others.

A panel model is constructed to explore the factors determining the development of insurance markets in the EU. The model explains the evolution of density rate depending on seven independent variables:

- GDP – Gross Domestic Product (US Dollar, million), respectively, in constant price terms (2010)
- P – population
- N – number of insurance companies
- SL – share of life insurance in total market (life gross written premium/total gross written premium) (%)
- RR – retention rate (%)
- FL – share of foreign insurance companies (Life) (%)
- FNL – share of foreign insurance companies (Non-life) (%)

The insurance markets of all the EU countries are examined regardless of the dates of their joining or leaving the EU – 28 countries. The period 1999–2019 is studied. Annual financial data from the following databases are utilised: EIOPA Database, 2021, Eurostat Database, 2021, OECD Statistics, 2021 and Insurance Europe, 2021.

The key descriptive statistics that characterise the variables are shown in Table 2.10 and Figure 2.8.

An analysis of the basic descriptive statistics of the variables studied demonstrates the following:

- They are internally diverse. This is indicated by variance and standard deviation, which represent the dispersion around the mean.
- The average GDP is 661,841.094; yet, its minimum is 9959.267 and the maximum value is 4,170,262.51, evidence of a large variability of the countries reviewed in respect of economic development.
- The average population is 17,891,604, but its minimum is 379,360 and the maximum value is 83,019,213, evidence of a large variability of the countries reviewed in respect of population.

Table 2.10 Basic statistics concerning the variables studied of EU insurance market development in 1999–2019

Specification	*GDP*	*P*	*DR*	*N*	*SL*	*RR*	*FL*	*FNL*
N importance	588	588	588	588	588	588	588	588
Average	661,841.094	17,891,604	2981.793	146.8231	47.34516	86.30004	45.32445	43.22136
Median	283,935.907	8,858,327	1238.763	63.00000	46.21950	88.35950	39.70900	43.01100
Maximum	4,170,262.51	83,019,213	54,329.32	777.0000	94.28600	113.0700	100.0000	100.0000
Minimum	9959.267	379,360	10.54200	12.00000	12.74800	48.63800	0.00	0.118000
Variance	8.813240E+11	5.136039E+14	44,366,647	24,997.28	367.3550	92.30135	1177.782	917.2013
Standard deviation	938,788.6	22,662,831	6660.829	158.1053	19.16651	9.607359	34.31882	30.28533

Source: The authors' own research on STATISTICA 12.

Explanation: GDP – Gross Domestic Product (US Dollar, million), respectively, in constant price terms (2010); P – population; DR – density rate – gross written premium/population (US Dollar); N – number of insurance companies; SL – share of life insurance in total market (life gross written premium/total gross written premium) (%); RR – retention rate (%); FL – share of foreign insurance companies (Life) (%); FNL – share of foreign insurance companies (Non-life) (%).

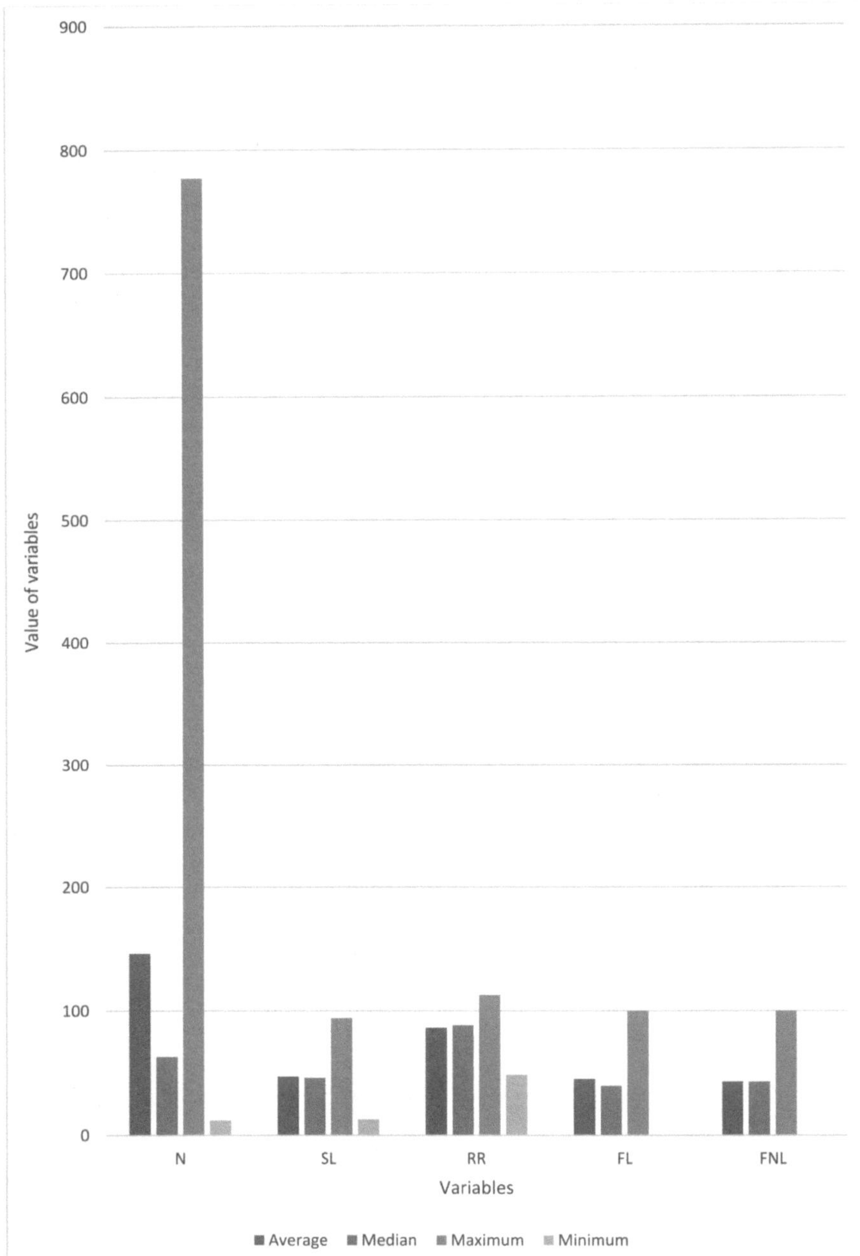

Figure 2.8 Selected basic statistics concerning the variables studied of EU insurance market development in 1999–2019.

- The average density rate is 2981.793 but its minimum is 10.542 and the maximum value is 54,329.32, evidence of a large variability of the countries reviewed in respect of the development of the insurance market.
- The average number of insurance companies is 146.8231 but its minimum is 12 and the maximum value is 777, evidence of a large variability of the countries reviewed in respect of the number of insurance companies.
- The average share of life insurance in total market is 47.34516 but its minimum is 2.748 and the maximum value is 94.286, evidence of a large variability of the countries reviewed in respect of the development of life insurance.
- The average retention rate is 86.30004 (average) but its minimum is 48.638 and the maximum value is 113.07, evidence of a large variability of the countries reviewed in respect of reinsurance.
- The average share of foreign life insurance companies is 45.32445 but its minimum is 0.00 and the maximum value is 100.00, evidence of a large variability of the countries reviewed in respect of the share of foreign capital in the insurance market.
- The average share of foreign non-life insurance companies is 43.22136 but its minimum is 0.118 and its maximum value is 100.00, evidence of a large variability of the variable.

Causes of the large divergences of the variables examined should be sought both in the extensive group of the countries studied and in their significant diversity in terms of economic development, the development of insurance markets and the relatively long research period, as proven by the key statistic of the variables studied – hence the high differences between the minimum and maximum values of the variables reviewed.

Table 2.11 contains a matrix of correlations among the variables.

The model presented below is constructed by means of backward stepwise regression.

$$lnDR_{i,t} = a_1 + a_2 lnGDPp_{i,t} + a_3 lnSL_{i,t} + a_4 lnRR_{i,t} + a_5 \Delta N_{i,t} + u_{i,t}, \tag{2.1}$$

where

$DR_{i,t}$ – density rate – gross written premium/population (US Dollar)
$GDPp_{i,t}$ – GDP per capita – GDP/population (US Dollar)
$SL_{i,t}$ – share of life insurance in total market (life gross written premium/ total gross written premium)
$RR_{i,t}$ – retention rate (retention of insurance premium)
$N_{i,t}$ – number of insurance companies
ln – natural logarithm
Δ – the operator of first differences
$u_{i,t}$ – joint random factor

Table 2.11 Correlation matrix of variables characterising the development of UE insurance markets in 1999–2019

Specification	*GDP*	*P*	*DR*	*N*	*SL*	*RR*	*FL*	*FNL*
GDP	1.000000	0.977069	−0.009067	0.773821	0.227991	0.180380	−0.433311	−0.377062
P	0.977069	1.000000	−0.056377	0.731448	0.187921	0.155799	−0.388384	−0.326975
DR	−0.009067	−0.056377	1.000000	0.361628	0.576952	−0.078387	0.021876	−0.096671
N	0.773821	0.731448	0.361628	1.000000	0.521037	0.154663	−0.492094	−0.445977
SL	0.227991	0.187921	0.576952	0.521037	1.000000	0.189152	−0.380783	−0.266132
RR	0.180380	0.155799	−0.078387	0.154663	0.189152	1.000000	−0.177179	−0.181960
FL	−0.433311	−0.388384	0.021876	−0.492094	−0.380783	−0.177179	1.000000	0.853722
FNL	−0.377062	−0.326975	−0.096671	−0.445977	−0.266132	−0.181960	0.853722	1.000000

Source: The authors' own research on STATISTICA 12.

Explanation: GDP – Gross Domestic Product (US Dollar, million), respectively, in constant price terms (2010); P – population; DR – density rate – gross written premium/population (US Dollar); N – number of insurance companies; SL – share of life insurance in total market (life gross written premium/total gross written premium) (%); RR – retention rate (%); FL – share of foreign insurance companies (Life) (%); FNL – share of foreign insurance companies (Non-life) (%).

Table 2.12 Model estimation: WLS, using 560 observations

	Coefficient	*Std. Error*	*t-ratio*	*p-value*	
Const.	−21.4776	0.544230	−39.46	<0.0001	***
l GDPp	2.78499	0.0496891	56.05	<0.0001	***
l SL	0.606546	0.0466201	13.01	<0.0001	***
d N	−0.00036639	0.000613323	−0.5974	0.5505	
l RR	0.323834	0.134700	2.404	0.0165	**

Statistics based on the weighted data:			
Sum squared resid	547.4783	S.E. of regression	0.993201
R-squared	0.923286	Adjusted R-squared	0.922733
F(4, 555)	1669.909	p-value (F)	9.2e–308
Log-likelihood	−788.2737	Akaike criterion	1586.547
Schwarz criterion	1608.187	Hannan-Quinn	1594.997
Statistics based on the original data:			
Mean dependent var.	6.949473	S.D. dependent var.	1.504891
Sum squared resid	127.5705	S.E. of regression	0.479434
Test for normality of residual:			
Null hypothesis:		error is normally distributed	
Test statistic:		Chi-square(2) = 5.55489	
		with p-value = 0.0621973	

Source: The authors' own research on GRETL.

Included 28 cross-sectional units. Dependent variable: L_DR. Weights based on per-unit error variances

Explanation: *** The variable is significant at the significance level of 0.01; ** The variable is significant at the significance level of 0.05; * The variable is significant at the significance level of 0.1.

The model estimation with the classic least-squares method and testing detect the presence of heteroscedasticity and autocorrelation. Some attempts at the model estimation with fixed and random effects suggest an autocorrelation of residues as well. Finally, the estimation employs the method of Weighted Least Squares (WSL). The results are included in Table 2.12.

The results of the model estimation show that all the dependent variables are statistically significant. The model explains 92% of the variability of the dependent variable. The share of life assurance in the insurance market and the retention have quite strong effects on the changes of the dependent variable.

This study shows, therefore, that the development of insurance markets in the EU countries studied in 1999–2019 was statistically significantly influenced by the level of economic development measured with GDP per capita, the share of life insurance in the total market and the level of reinsurance, represented with the retention rate.

The insurance market development and economic growth in the EU – An econometric analysis

The problem of relations between the development of insurance and economic growth is becoming more and more popular. Three groups of relations are possible which point to the directions of impact of the insurance market development on economic growth:

- Demand-following – the development of insurance affects economic growth. This is confirmed by Arena (2008), Haiss and Sümegi (2008) and Bednarczyk (2012), inter alia.
- Supply-leading – economic growth influences the development of insurance, as corroborated by the studies of, among others, Dash *et al.* (2018), Wang and Lee (2018), Tian *et al.* (2018) and Ostrowska-Dankiewicz and Simionescu (2020).
- Feedback – a two-way relation upheld by Burić *et al.* (2017) and Dash *et al.* (2018), among other research.

The insurance markets of the particular countries develop under the influence of various factors. The literature commonly distinguishes three categories of factors affecting the insurance market: economic (GNP, employment, inflation, etc.), demographic (age, gender, education and the like) and social (aversion to risk, education, religion, etc.). This is affirmed by Sen and Madheswaran (2013), Sen (2007), Hwang and Greenford (2005), Beck and Webb (2003) and Zietz (2003), inter alia.

The existence of a dependence between the development of insurance markets and economic growth is the research problem. A panel model is constructed to explore this dependence in the EU countries. The model explains the evolution of GDP as dependent on nine independent variables:

- P – population
- WP – gross written premium (US Dollar, million)
- N – number of insurance companies
- DR – density rate – gross written premium/population (US Dollar)
- PR – penetration rate – gross written premium/GDP (%)
- SL – share of life insurance in total market (life gross written premium/total gross written premium)
- RR – retention rate
- FL – share of foreign insurance companies (Life)
- FNL – share of foreign insurance companies (Non-life)

The insurance markets of all the EU countries are studied regardless of the date of joining or leaving the EU – 28 countries. The years 1999–2019 are covered. Annual financial data from the following databases are utilised: EIOPA Database, 2021, Eurostat Database, 2021, OECD Statistics, 2021 and Insurance Europe, 2021.

The key descriptive statistics that characterise the variables are shown in Table 2.13 and Figure 2.9.

Table 2.13 Basic statistics concerning the variables studied of EU insurance market development and economic growth in 1999–2019

Specification	*GDP*	*P*	*WP*	*N*	*DR*	*PR*	*SL*	*RR*	*FL*	*FNL*
N importance	588	588	588	588	588	588	588	588	588	588
Average	661,841.094	17,891,604	49,497	146.8231	2981.793	6.608479	47.34516	86.30004	45.32445	43.22136
Median	283,935.907	8,858,327	8033	63.00000	1238.763	5.098500	46.21950	88.35950	39.70900	43.01100
Maximum	4,170,262.51	83,019,213	644,557	777.0000	54,329.32	51.20400	94.28600	113.0700	100.0000	100.0000
Minimum	9959.267	379,360	95.7	12.00000	10.54200	0.753000	12.74800	48.63800	0.00	0.118000
Variance	8.813240E+11	5.136039E+14	9.110067E+09	24,997.28	44,366,647	44.77260	367.3550	92.30135	1177.782	917.2013
Standard deviation	938,788.6	22,662,831	95,447	158.1053	6660.829	6.691233	19.16651	9.607359	34.31882	30.28533

Source: The authors' own research on STATISTICA 12.

Explanation: GDP – Gross Domestic Product (US Dollar, million), respectively, in constant price terms (2010); P – population; WP – gross written premium (US Dollar, million); N – number of insurance companies; DR – density rate – gross written premium/population (US Dollar); PR – penetration rate – gross written premium/GDP (%); SL – share of life insurance in total market (life gross written premium/total gross written premium); RR – retention rate; FL – share of foreign insurance companies (Life); FNL – share of foreign insurance companies (Non-life).

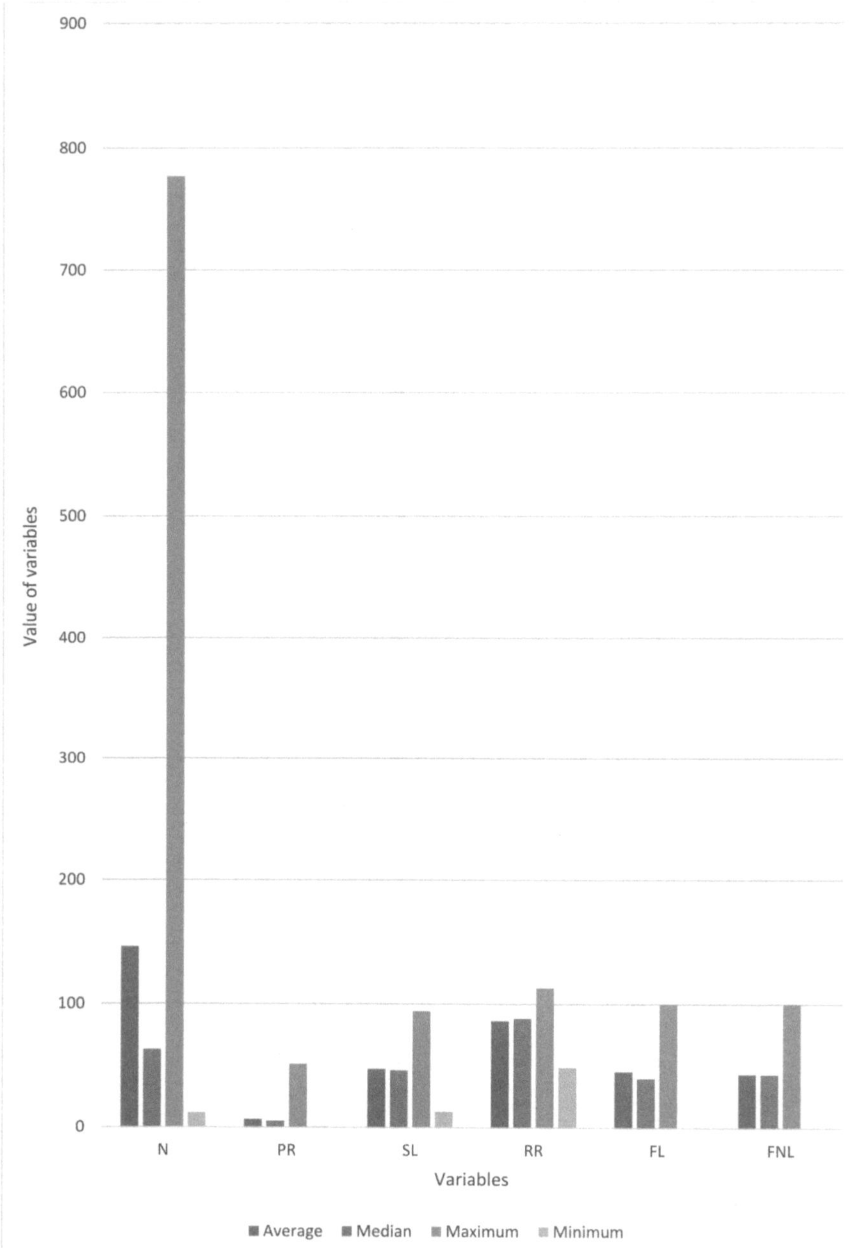

Figure 2.9 Selected basic statistics concerning the variables studied of EU insurance market development and economic growth in 1999–2019.

An analysis of the basic descriptive statistics of the variables studied demonstrates:

- They are internally diverse. This is indicated by variance and standard deviation, which represent the dispersion around the mean.
- The average GDP is 661,841.094; yet, its minimum is 9959.267 and the maximum value is 4,170,262.51, evidence of a large variability of the countries reviewed in respect of economic development.
- The average population is 17,891,604; yet, its minimum is 379,360 and the maximum value is 83,019,213, evidence of a large variability of the countries reviewed in respect of their population.
- The average gross written premium is US$49,497 million but its minimum is US$95.7 million and the maximum value is US$83,019,213 million, evidence of a large variability of the insurance markets reviewed.
- The average number of insurance companies is 146.8231; yet, its minimum is 12 and the maximum value is 777, evidence of a large variability of the size of insurance markets.
- The average density rate is 2981.793; yet, its minimum is 10.542 and the maximum value is 54,329.32, evidence of a large variability of the countries reviewed in respect of the development of insurance markets.
- The average penetration rate is 6.608479; yet, its minimum is 0.753 and the maximum value is 51.204, evidence of a large variability of the countries reviewed in respect of the significance of their insurance sectors.
- The average share of life insurance in the total market is 47.34516; yet, its minimum is 12.748 and the maximum value is 94.286, evidence of a large variability of the countries reviewed in respect of their life insurance's development.
- The average retention rate is 86.30004; yet, its minimum is 48.638 and the maximum value is 113.07, evidence of a large variability of the utilisation of reinsurance.
- The average share of foreign life insurance companies is 45.32445; yet, its minimum is 0.00 and the maximum value is 100.00, evidence of a large variability of the shares of foreign capital in insurance markets.
- The average share of foreign non-life insurance companies is 43.22136; yet, its minimum is 0.118 and the maximum value is 100.00, evidence of a large variability of the variable studied.

Causes of the large divergences of the variables examined should be sought both in the extensive group of the countries studied and in their significant diversity in terms of economic development, the development of insurance markets and the relatively long research period, which was varied, as proven by the key statistic of the variables studied – hence the high differences between the minimum and maximum values of the variables reviewed.

Table 2.14 contains a matrix of correlations among the variables.

Table 2.14 Correlation matrix of variables characterising the development of insurance markets and economic growth of EU countries in 1999–2019

Specification	*P*	*GDP*	*WP*	*N*	*DR*	*PR*	*SL*	*RR*	*FL*	*FNL*
P	1.000000	0.977069	0.842093	0.731448	−0.056377	0.042686	0.187921	0.155799	−0.388384	−0.326975
GDP	0.977069	1.000000	0.891446	0.773821	−0.009067	0.101588	0.227991	0.180380	−0.433311	−0.377062
WP	0.842093	0.891446	1.000000	0.771109	0.103482	0.245031	0.318712	0.135433	−0.405955	−0.343193
N	0.731448	0.773821	0.771109	1.000000	0.361628	0.509817	0.521037	0.154663	−0.492094	−0.445977
DR	−0.056377	−0.009067	0.103482	0.361628	1.000000	0.925809	0.576952	−0.078387	0.021876	−0.096671
PR	0.042686	0.101588	0.245031	0.509817	0.925809	1.000000	0.711191	−0.042367	−0.177640	−0.252608
SL	0.187921	0.227991	0.318712	0.521037	0.576952	0.711191	1.000000	0.189152	−0.380783	−0.266132
RR	0.155799	0.180380	0.135433	0.154663	−0.078387	−0.042367	0.189152	1.000000	−0.177179	−0.181960
FL	−0.388384	−0.433311	−0.405955	−0.492094	0.021876	−0.177640	−0.380783	−0.177179	1.000000	0.853722
FNL	−0.326975	−0.377062	−0.343193	−0.445977	−0.096671	−0.252608	−0.266132	−0.181960	0.853722	1.000000

Source: The authors' own research on STATISTICA 12.

Explanation: P – population; GDP – Gross Domestic Product (US Dollar, million), respectively, in constant price terms (2010); WP – gross written premium (US Dollar, million); N – number of insurance companies; DR – density rate – gross written premium/population (US Dollar); PR – penetration rate – gross written premium/GDP (%); SL – share of life insurance in total market (life gross written premium/total gross written premium); RR – retention rate; FL – share of foreign insurance companies (Life); FNL – share of foreign insurance companies (Non-life).

The model presented below is constructed by means of backward stepwise regression.

$$lnGDP_{i,t} = a_1 + a_2 lnWP_{i,t} + a_3 lnF_{i,t} + a_4 lnP_{i,t} + u_{i,t}, \quad (2.2)$$

where

$GDP_{i,t}$ – Gross Domestic Product (US Dollar, million), respectively, in constant price terms (2010)
$WP_{i,t}$ – gross written premium (US Dollar, million)
$F_{i,t}$ – share of foreign insurance companies in the market
$P_{i,t}$ – population
ln – natural logarithm
$u_{i,t}$ – joint random factor

The model estimation with the classic least-squares method and testing detect the presence of heteroscedasticity and autocorrelation. Some attempts at the model estimation with fixed and random effects suggest an autocorrelation of residues as well. Finally, the estimation employs the method of WSL. The results are included in Table 2.15.

The results of the model estimation show that all the dependent variables are statistically significant. The model explains 99% of the variability of the

Table 2.15 Model estimation: WLS, using 588 observations

	Coefficient	*Std. Error*	*t-ratio*	*p-value*	
Const.	8.83088	0.0592742	149.0	<0.0001	***
l WP	0.275474	0.00373243	73.81	<0.0001	***
l F	0.0165215	0.00353868	4.669	<0.0001	***
l P	0.704270	0.00531805	132.4	<0.0001	***
Statistics based on the weighted data:					
Sum squared resid		577.9118	S.E. of regression		0.994774
R-squared		0.994946	Adjusted R-squared		0.994920
F(3, 584)		38319.73	p-value (F)		0.000000
Log-likelihood		−829.2480	Akaike criterion		1666.496
Schwarz criterion		1684.003	Hannan-Quinn		1673.317
Statistics based on the original data:					
Mean dependent var		26.26912	S.D. dependent var		1.464699
Sum squared resid		11.24055	S.E. of regression		0.138735
Test for normality of residual:					
Null hypothesis:			error is normally distributed		
Test statistic:			Chi-square (2) = 2.81262 with p-value = 0.245046		

Source: The authors' own research on GRETL.

Included 28 cross-sectional units. Dependent variable: L_GDP. Weights based on per-unit error variances

Explanation: *** The variable is significant at the significance level of 0.01; ** The variable is significant at the significance level of 0.05; * The variable is significant at the significance level of 0.1.

dependent variable. The rate of written premium growth has quite a strong impact on the changes of the dependent variable.

This study of the EU countries in 1999–2019 proves, therefore, that the economic growth measured with the GDP is affected by the variables characterising the development of insurance markets. The economic growth is statistically significantly influenced by gross written premium, the share of foreign insurance companies in the market and population.

Conclusion

This research, concerning the development of the EU countries' insurance markets in 1999–2019, shows that they vary in their sizes, structures and significance to the national economies. In general, they can be divided into the insurance markets of the EU-15 and the remaining EU member states. The insurance markets of the EU-15 countries are characterised by a greater number of insurers, the prevalence of life assurance and the rates describing both their development and significance to national economies which are distinctly better than in the remaining member countries. The higher level of economic development, as well as the sizes and populations of the countries are undoubtedly contributing factors. The date of joining the EU seems a major factor determining the level of insurance market development. This is corroborated by an analysis of insurance markets in the remaining EU member states. The markets of the countries that joined the EU earlier (e.g., Poland and Slovakia) display better parameters than of those which joined later (e.g., Bulgaria and Romania).

A review of factors determining the development of insurance markets in the EU countries in 1999–2019 proves that the overall level of economic development of a given country was the crucial contributor. This means the higher the level of economic development, the better the parameters characterising a given insurance market and suggesting its more advanced development. The share of life assurance is another major factor in the development of insurance markets. Generally speaking, the more developed an insurance market, the greater the share of life insurance. This should be related to both economic factors indicating a higher welfare of a given society and sociological factors that suggest more confidence in the insurance sector. The standard of reinsurance is another factor determining the development of the insurance markets examined. The greater the retention rate, the better developed an insurance market. This may be the evidence of more capital available to insurance companies but also a consequence of the market structure – a larger share of life assurance, where reinsurance is more rarely applied.

An analysis of the impact of insurance market development on the economic growth of the EU countries in 1999–2019 demonstrates that there is such a dependence. The study identified three statistically significant determinants of economic growth in the countries examined: gross written premium, the share of foreign capital and population. The insurance premium is the crucial determinant of insurance market development that influences economic growth, therefore. Both the population and the share of foreign capital appear universal factors of economic growth, attributable to most sectors of the economy.

Notes

1. From 2007 EU member.
2. From 2013 EU member.
3. From 2004 EU member.
4. From 2004 EU member.
5. From 2004 EU member.
6. From 2004 EU member.
7. From 2004 EU member.
8. From 2004 EU member.
9. From 2004 EU member.
10. From 2004 EU member.
11. From 2007 EU member.
12. From 2004 EU member.
13. From 2004 EU member.
14. From 2020 leaving the EU.
15. From 2007 EU member.
16. From 2013 EU member.
17. From 2004 EU member.
18. From 2004 EU member.
19. From 2004 EU member.
20. From 2004 EU member.
21. From 2004 EU member.
22. From 2004 EU member.
23. From 2004 EU member.
24. From 2004 EU member.
25. From 2007 EU member.
26. From 2004 EU member.
27. From 2004 EU member.
28. From 2020 leaving the EU.
29. From 2007 EU member.
30. From 2013 EU member.
31. From 2004 EU member.
32. From 2004 EU member.
33. From 2004 EU member.
34. From 2004 EU member.
35. From 2004 EU member.
36. From 2004 EU member.
37. From 2004 EU member.
38. From 2004 EU member.
39. From 2007 EU member.
40. From 2004 EU member.
41. From 2004 EU member.
42. From 2020 leaving the EU.
43. From 2007 EU member.
44. From 2013 EU member.
45. From 2004 EU member.

46. From 2004 EU member.
47. From 2004 EU member.
48. From 2004 EU member.
49. From 2004 EU member.
50. From 2004 EU member.
51. From 2004 EU member.
52. From 2004 EU member.
53. From 2007 EU member.
54. From 2004 EU member.
55. From 2004 EU member.
56. From 2020 leaving the EU.

Bibliography

Arena, M., 2008. Does insurance market promote economic growth? A cross-country study for industrialized and developing countries. *Journal of Risk and Insurance*, 75 (4), pp. 921–946. doi.org/10.1111/j.1539-6975.2008.00291.x.

Beck, T. & Webb, I., 2003. Economic, demographic and institutional determinants of life insurance consumption. *The World Bank Economic Review*, 17 (1), pp. 51–88.

Bednarczyk, T., 2012. *Wpływ działalności sektora ubezpieczeniowego na wzrost gospodarczy*. Lublin: Wydawnictwo Uniwersytetu Marii Curie-Skłodowskiej.

Brokešová, Z. & Vachálková, I., 2016. Macroeconomic environment and insurance industry development: The case of Visegrad group countries. *Central European Review of Economic Issues. Economická Revue*, 19, pp. 63–72.

Browne, M. J. & Kim, K., 1993. An international analysis of life insurance demand. *The Journal of Risk and Insurance*, 60 (4), pp. 616–634. doi.org/10.2307/253382.

Bukowski, S. I. & Lament, M., 2019. Impact of foreign capital on the insurance market development in the Visegrad group countries. *Journal of Management and Financial Sciences*, XII (38), pp. 33–45.

Bukowski, S. I. & Lament, M., 2020. Foreign capital impact on insurance market development in EU-15 countries. *Entrepreneurial Business and Economics Review*, 8 (3), pp. 205–219. doi:10.15678/EBER.2020.080312.

Bukowski, S. I. & Lament, M., 2021a. Market structure and financial effectiveness of life insurance companies. *European Research Studies Journal*, XXIV (2B), pp. 533–545. doi: 10.35808/ersj/2248.

Bukowski, S. I. & Lament, M., 2021b. Business model impact on the financial efficiency of insurance companies. *European Research Studies Journal*, XXIV (Special Issue 4), pp. 237–247. doi: 10.35808/ersj/2685.

Burić, M. N., Smolović, J. C., Božović, M. L. & Filipović, A. L., 2017. Impact of economic factors on life insurance development in Western Balkan countries. *Zbornik radova Ekonomskog fakulteta u Rijeci: časopis za ekonomsku teoriju i praksu*, 35 (2), pp. 21–38.

Carson, J. M., Chen, P. H. & Outreville, J. F., 2014. Does foreign direct investment affect the supply of life insurance in developing countries? Retrieved from http://citeseerx.ist.psu.edu/viewdoc/download?doi=10.1.1.684.9911&rep=rep1&type=pdf on June 5, 2018.

Chui, A. C. & Kwok, C. C., 2008. National culture and life insurance consumption. *Journal of International Business Studies*, 39 (1), pp. 88–101. doi.org/10.1057/palgrave.jibs.8400316.

Cristian, B. C., 2010. Current coordinates of the Romanian insurance sector. *Annals of Faculty of Economics*, 1 (2), pp. 504–508.

Dash, S., Pradhan, R. P., Maradana, R. P., Gaurav, K., Zaki, D. B. & Jayakumar, M., 2018. Insurance market penetration and economic growth in Eurozone countries: Time series evidence causality. *Future Business Journal*, 4, pp. 50–67. doi: 10.1016/j.fbj.2017.11.005.

Ducháčková, E. & Daňhel, J., 2006. Postavení zemí V4 na pojistném trhu Evropské unie. In: *Competitivness in the EU – Challenge for the V4 Countries*, Nitra: SPU.

Ducháčková, E. & Daňhel, J., 2010. *Teorie pojistných trhů*. Praha: Professional Publishing.

EIOPA Database. 2021. Retrieved from https://www.eiopa.europa.eu/tools-and-data/statistics-and-risk-dashboards/insurance-statistics_en on July 15, 2021.

Eurostat Database. 2021. Retrieved from https://ec.europa.eu/eurostat/web/main/data/database on August 15, 2021.

Haiss, P. & Sümegi, K., 2008. The relationship between insurance and economic growth in Europe: A theoretical and empirical analysis. *Empirica*, 35 (4), pp. 405–431. doi.org/10.1007/s10663-008-9075-2.

Han, L., Li, D., Moshirian, F. & Tian, Y., 2010. Insurance development and economic growth. *Geneva Papers on Risk and Insurance*, 35 (1), pp. 183–199. doi.org/10.1057/gpp.2010.4.

Hwang, T. & Greenford, B., 2005. A cross-section analysis of the determinants of life insurance consumption in Mainland China, Hong Kong, and Taiwan. *Risk Management and Insurance Review*, 8 (1), pp. 103–125. doi.org/10.1111/j.1540-6296.2005.00051.x.

Insurance Europe. 2021. Retrieved from https://www.insuranceeurope.eu/statistics on August 15, 2021.

Isik, O., 2021. Analysing the determinants of profitability of domestic and foreign non-life insurers in Turkey. *International Journal of Insurance and Finance*, pp. 45–55. doi: 10.52898/ijif.2021.5.

Kurylo, V., Kurylo, L., Zhovnirchyk, Y., Kartashov, Y. & Sokol, S., 2017. The development of the insurance market of Ukraine amid the global trends in insurance. *Investment Management and Financial Innovations*, 14 (1), pp. 14–27. doi.org/10.21511/imfi.14(1-1).2017.07.

Li, D., Moshirian, F., Nguyen, P. & Wee, T., 2007. The demand for life insurance in OECD countries. *The Journal of Risk and Insurance*, 74 (3), pp. 637–652. doi.org/10.1111/j.1539-6975.2007.00228.x.

Medveď, D. & Kavčič, S., 2012. An empirical study of efficiency in Croatia and Slovenia insurance markets. *Ekonomska istraživanja*, 25 (1), pp. 105–120.

Munir, K. & Ameer, A., 2018. Effect of economic growth, trade openness, urbanization, and technology on environment of Asian emerging economies. *Management of Environmental Quality: An International Journal*, 29 (6), pp. 1123–1134.

Mutairi, A. A. L., Naser, H. & Naser, K., 2021. Determinants of corporate performance: Empirical evidence from the insurance companies listed on Abu Dhabi securities exchange (ADX). *Accounting*, 7, pp. 143–150. doi: 10.5267/j.ac.2020.10.003.

OECD Statistics. 2021. Insurance Statistics. Retrieved from https://stats.oecd.org on August 15, 2021.

Ostrowska-Dankiewicz, A. & Simionescu, M., 2020. Relationship between the insurance market and macroeconomic indicators in the EU member states. *Transformations in Business & Economics*, 19 (51), pp. 175–187.

Outreville, J. F., 1990. The economic significant of insurance markets in developing countries. *Journal of Risk and Insurance*, 18 (3), pp. 487–498.

Pye, R., 2005. The evolution of financial services in transition economies: An overview of the insurance sector. *Post-Communist Economies*, 17 (2), pp. 205–223.

Sankaramuthukumar, S. & Alamelu, K., 2012. A SWOT analysis of Sri Lankan insurance sector. *The Journal of Risk and Insurance*, 9 (1), pp. 27–47.

Sen, S. 2007. Are life insurance demand determinants valid for selected Asian economies and India?, Institute for Social and Economic Change. Paper for Presentation at Annual Meeting of APRIA, [Internet], pp. 1–27, Retrieved from https://www.scribd.com/document/230968492/13507Paper-APRIA-Subir-Draft on October 15, 2018.

Sen, S. & Madheswaran, S., 2013. Regional determinants of life insurance consumption: Evidence from selected Asian economies. *Asian-Pacific Economic Literature*, 27 (2), pp. 86–103. doi.org/10.1111/apel.12024.

Sun, J., Wang, J., Wang, T. & Zhang, T., 2019. Urbanization, economic growth, and environmental pollution: Partial differential analysis based on the spatial Durbin model. *Management of Environmental Quality: An International Journal*, 30 (2), pp. 483–494.

Swiss Re, 2011. World insurance in 2010. Premiums back to growth – Capital increases, Swiss Re Institute, Sigma 2/2011.

Swiss Re, 2017. World insurance in 2016: the China growth engine steams ahead, Swiss Re Institute, Sigma 3/2017.

Swiss Re, 2020. World insurance: Riding out the 2020 pandemic storm, Swiss Re Institute, Sigma 4/2020.

Swiss Re, 2021. Turbulence after lift-off: global economic and insurance market outlook 2022/23, Swiss Re Institute, Sigma 5/2021.

Tian, L., Jiang, S. J., Pan, G. & Zhang, N., 2018. Non-life insurance price dynamics: Evidence from the Chinese insurance market. *Economic Research-Ekonomska Istraživanja*, 31 (1), pp. 171–187. doi.org/10.1080/1331677X.2018.1424557.

Wang, K. M. & Lee, Y. M., 2018. The impacts of life insurance asymmetrically on health expenditure and economic growth: Dynamic panel threshold approach. *Economic Research-Ekonomska Istraživanja*, 31 (1), pp. 440–460. doi.org/10.1080/1331677X.2018.1429943.

Ward, D. & Zurbruegg, R., 2002. Does insurance promote economic growth? Evidence from OECD countries. *Journal of Risk and Insurance*, 67 (4), pp. 489–506.

Zhang, C. & Zhu, N., 2005. Determinants of the development of insurance in China under the globalization, Working Paper Centre D'Études et de Recherches sur le Dévelopement International. Retrieved from https://pdfs.semanticscholar.org/5b03/2f2e73daba3584185301f73be197250e7fe9.pdf on November 10, 2018.

Zheng, W., Liu, Y. & Deng, Y., 2009. A comparative study of international insurance sector. *The Geneva Papers on Risk and Insurance – Issues and Practice*, 34 (1), pp. 85–99. doi.org/10.1057/gpp.2008.37.

Zietz, E. N., 2003. An examination of the demand for life insurance. *Risk Management and Insurance Review*, 6 (2), pp. 159–191. doi.org/10.1046/J.1098-1616.2003.030.x.

3 Integration of financial markets in the Euro area

The definitions of financial market integration

The single financial market in the European Union (EU) is part of its single internal market. The freedoms of establishment, service provision and capital flows are the basic conditions of its operation. The integration of financial markets is a stage of financial integration. The following stages of financial integration can be distinguished:

a The liberalisation of capital flows (including the inflows of foreign direct investments, largely owing to transnational corporations).
b The integration of financial institutions and systems.
c Continued economic integration in the area of capital markets integration by introducing a single currency (Bekaert *et al.*, 1998, p. 34).

Thus, the financial integration includes the market liberalisation and an in-depth integration, also involving capital markets, until a single currency is adopted.

The financial integration of financial markets is generally taken to mean the liberalisation of capital flows, the harmonisation of tax and budgetary systems, the unifications of banking and financial institutions, and the integration of capital markets (Zabielski, 1999, p. 111).

The integration of financial markets has been noted for more than two decades, driven by some processes in the world economy. For Europe, the introduction of a currency shared by the EU countries, the Euro, in 1999 was an especially important factor fostering the integration. The process of integration in the European financial markets has coincided with the worldwide tendency to globalisation and an increasing significance of securitisation stimulated by a liberalisation of international capital flows, the lifting of administrative restrictions to financial markets (deregulation), as well as the development of IT and telecommunications (see Stirbu, 2004, p. 7).

The integration of financial markets in the EU means, on the one hand, the provision for free capital and financial service flows within the EU, or

DOI: 10.4324/9781003227762-3

the formation of a single market out of the particular countries' financial markets. This type of integration is known as the transborder integration of financial markets. The integration of financial markets also denotes the joining of entities active in various sectors of the financial market as part of the single market, e.g., banks, insurance companies and other financial intermediaries by way of establishing financial conglomerates, on the other hand. This is the so-called intersectoral integration.

The integration of financial markets may be defined narrowly. This definition is grounded in the law of one price. Thus, the integration of financial markets is a realisation of that law. This means that assets generating identical cash flows have the same price (rate of return). As a result, if firms issue bonds in two countries or regions, they must pay the same rate of interest to bond holders from both the countries (regions). Similarly, in the case of shares in two countries (regions), the price of capital obtained in the financial market through share issues should be identical. If this line of thinking is applied to the credit and deposit market, households should be able to borrow on the same terms in both the countries (regions) regardless of where their bank is based (cf. Adam et al., 2002, p. 4).

However, an application of the foregoing definition to research into the process of financial market integration on an international scale would narrow the field of study to markets where the principles of financial instrument issue and pricing are standardised. Internationally, though, there are a number of deviations from the law of one price, for instance, by means of restrictions that exclude certain financial instruments from trading in some countries. Thus, financial markets are not integrated to identical extents. Hence, L. Baele *et al.* formulate a broader definition of integrated financial markets (Baele *et al.*, 2004, pp. 6–7): "a market of some financial instruments and/or services is fully integrated if all potential market users of identical characteristics:

a Are subject to the same rules once they decide to take part in trading in these financial instruments and/or services.
b Have identical access to these instruments and/or services.
c Are treated identically when they operate in the market".

This broad take on the integration of financial markets implies the law of one price as well. This law states that assets are characterised by identical risks and returns. If the law of one price is not fulfilled, there is room for arbitration that restores the validity of the law (provided there are no barriers to the integration of financial markets discussed below) (see Baele *et al.*, 2004, p. 7).

Both the definitions describe the state of affairs. However, they can become points of reference for the assessment of the integration processes of financial markets and of the degree of that integration (see also Bukowski, 2011, p. 29; Bukowski, 2020, p. 24).

The foregoing discussion shows that the integration of financial markets is a complex issue, because it is a stage of financial integration and given the extent of integration, it affects the entire world and its various regions, e.g., the EU. In practice, the scope and degree of the integration vary and are often dependent on regulatory activities; what matters to the growth of integration is whether they address the inflows of foreign direct investments (Bekaert *et al.*, 1998, p. 34).

Globalisation and barriers to the financial market integration on an international scale

The globalisation of financial markets denotes their integration on the global scale as part of the world economy, and thus greater interdependences between the stock exchange cycle and the development of stock indices of returns on financial assets. It should be noted, though, that consolidation processes primarily take place at national levels and are determined by factors like the size of national economies, legal regulations, fiscal systems and cultural and social differences. The degree to which financial markets of individual countries are integrated into the global market varies and depends on the following factors:

a The degree to which an economy is open.
b The rate of exchange system.
c The degree to which capital flows are liberalised.
d The degree to which a given country's economy is integrated into the global economy and/or the economies of other countries as part of regional integration.
e The degree to which the boom and bust cycle in a given country is synchronised with the cycle abroad.
f The involvement of transnational corporations in an economy.
g The degree to which an economy is internationalised.
h The degree of internationalisation of the financial sector, including stock exchanges, in a given country.
i The size of the financial market in a given country and its significance to the world and regional economy.
j Progress on Information and Communication Technologies (ICT) in a given country.
k The development of financial engineering and its application to the financial market of a given country.

The same factors apply to the integration of financial markets in integrating groups, in particular, monetary unions. A monetary union means a liquidation of most economic barriers to the integration of financial markets.

Financial markets are the more integrated, the less liable they are to local, idiosyncratic shocks, and the more exposed to the signals shared by a whole group of countries, an integrated grouping or the global economy they are (see Bukowski, 2020, pp. 25–26). According to Biegun (2015), a greater degree of financial integration helps to adapt an economy to asymmetric shocks.

A full integration of financial markets on an international scale encounters a range of barriers that prevent a complete equalisation of prices (rates of return) of financial assets.

Three groups of such barriers can be distinguished:

a Barriers related to economic policies, the operation of economies and financial markets.
b Barriers related to differences in commercial and financial legal systems.
c Barriers related to the presence of many currencies and non-harmonised international settlements of financial instrument transactions.

The first group of barriers comprises the effect of economic policy on capital flows and of international fiscal policy, different degrees of competitiveness among financial markets of the particular countries, differentiation of macroeconomic risk across countries and the asymmetry of information between foreign and domestic investors.

The policy of limiting access of foreign investors to a domestic market and restrictions to the flows of foreign capital are the fundamental and strongest barriers to financial integration on an international scale. Regulations applied to capital pricing (of interest rates, banking margins and commissions of financial intermediaries) are a major barrier. In addition, restrictions on trade in securities, composition of financial institutions' investment portfolios and access of foreign financial institutions to a domestic financial market play important roles in impeding financial integration and the development of financial markets. Bednarski and Polk (2019) see that the sources of the weak integration or fragmentation of the EU's financial sector can be found in overly restrictive prudential regulations that block free capital transfers and limit an optimum utilisation of financial liquidity within large, international banking groups.

The imperfect competitiveness of financial markets, exhibited in a limited competitiveness among financial institutions and poor transparency, produces differences of capital costs and high prices of financial intermediaries.

The competitiveness and macroeconomic stability of international economies and the stability of the socio-political environment vary. An international diversity of macroeconomic risk is a consequence that has a considerable impact on risk premium, the required rate of return and thus the directions and intensity of capital flows. The macroeconomic risk of an economy is substantially affected by fiscal policy. A growing budget deficit and the associated rising public debt enhance the macroeconomic risk. The research by F. Allen *et al.* (2013) corroborates that an increasing integration of financial markets helps to attain comparative advantage and risk diversification through international markets.

Various tax systems, systems of enterprise subsidies and of taxing income (or venue) from financial transactions, are commonly present in the particular countries. This varies the post-tax cost of capital.

The asymmetry of information between foreign and domestic investors is a major barrier. This is confirmed by A. Szypulewska-Porczyńska (2017). This barrier arises from the imperfection of financial markets, diffusion of information and the imperfect financial information flows internationally. It is associated with the cost of acquiring information about foreign financial markets (investment opportunities, investing and the possibilities of obtaining capital). This cost is normally not a problem for large enterprises, whereas it is often substantial for small- and medium-sized firms, and beyond the financial reach of households. These factors are a cause of home bias, which consists in investors tending to hold chiefly domestic financial assets in their portfolios.

The second group of barriers encompasses differences in regulations relevant to financial institutions and enterprises under corporate laws prevailing in the particular countries.

The barriers connected with the different systems of business law relate to the rules of corporate functioning, of floating financial instruments, or standards of accounting. It needs to be pointed out that the legal definitions of financial instruments (especially those in the monetary market) vary across countries and the regulations of the particular financial markets vary as a result, too.

All of this may heavily impede capital flows among countries and financial investments, discourage foreign investors and raise the costs of financial investments.

The presence of many currencies is one of the highest barriers to financial integration on an international scale. First, it generates the transactional costs of currency exchange. Second, the fluctuations of exchange rates lead to uncertainty as to the future developments of capital pricing, the costs of exchange risk and protection against that risk. As a consequence, capital pricing in different countries with their diverse currencies deviates from the pricing determined by international arbitration transactions. The cost of capital is also affected by the settlement costs of financial instrument transactions, since international settlement systems in this area are not harmonised.

These barriers can largely be lifted in a monetary union with a single currency (Bukowski, 2011, p. 37). One of the strongest barriers, multiple currencies, is liquidated above all. Second, the relatively low inflation proper to monetary union mechanisms, demonstrated with the experience of the Euro area, reduces the risk of inflation, of particular importance to investments in general and financial investments in particular. The problems with the free capital flows are absent. The macroeconomic risk in the individual union member countries diminishes. The systems of accounting and financial reporting are standardised. Fiscal systems become similar, although some differences persist, as the Euro experience shows. These differences are likely to continue for as long as a single fiscal policy is not introduced and key rules of taxation are not standardised (fiscal federalisation). The financial market regulations are subject to the same union principles, including that of a single licence for financial institutions. The degree of harmonisation of financial settlement systems increases internationally. The barriers likely to continue, with their effect cushioned in the long term, are the asymmetry of information and home bias, as well as the imperfect competitiveness of financial markets. They can be gradually overcome as the policy of a continuing economic and financial integration among the countries of a monetary union is realised.

The effect of economic shocks on a monetary union's economy should be remembered as well. The experience of the most recent financial and fiscal crisis and of the COVID-19 pandemic proves that their impact on the fragmentation of financial markets is considerable.

The processes of international financial integration have a positive influence over economic growth in a variety of its dimensions: of countries, regions, economic sectors and enterprises. The larger it is, the deeper the financial integration. For these reasons, attempts at fuller integration – both international, of regional integration groups, and individual countries – should continue. It should be stressed that the benefits from the integration of financial markets are not merely theoretical but are also upheld with empirical results, e.g., London Economics (2002), Guiso *et al.* (2004) and Thirlwalla (2006, pp. 240–241).

The measures of the degree of international market integration

The measures defined in the literature on financial integration can be divided into four major categories (see Pagano, 2002, p. 2):

1 The measures of credit and debt securities market integration.
2 The measures of share market integration.
3 The measures of integration based on economic decisions of households and enterprises.
4 The measures of institutional differences which may affect the segmentation of the financial market.

Four types of integration measures are distinguished in the group of the integration measures of the credit and debt securities market. The first relates to the differences of interest rates, e.g., for the interbank, debt, mortgage and corporate credit markets. The second type concerns the structure of investment portfolios of investment funds (in the cash and bond markets). Another group of measures applies to the differences of fees charged by banks for transborder transfers. The final group of measures relates to the numbers and shares of foreign banks in national markets. There are fewer measures of integration in the remaining three categories.

As far as the share market integration is concerned, the correlation of rates of returns on shares invested by institutional investors in foreign markets is adopted as the measure.

It's suggested that the conduct of households and enterprises be measured with the correlation between savings and investments, the correlation of consumption growth and the relation of transborder takeovers to national mergers and takeovers.

The assessment of institutional differences mainly consists in an analysis of domestic laws and their conformity to regional regulations (Pagano, 2002, pp. 4–5).

From the viewpoint of the financial market segments, the following measures of integration can be distinguished (see Bukowski, 2011, 2020, pp. 46–47):

1 The measures of monetary market.
2 The measures of credit and deposit market.
3 The measures of the treasury and corporate bond market.
4 The measures of share market.

From the perspective of the design of financial market integration indicators, which can be applied to virtually any segment of the financial market, the following are distinguished:

1 Price-based and field-based indicators.
2 News-based indicators.
3 Quantity-based indicators.

Some synthetic indicators of the financial market integration can be named, including:

1 Price-based financial integration composite indicator.
2 Quantity-based financial integration composite indicator.

The price-based financial integration composite indicator is designed by the selection of price-based indicators concerning four main segments of financial markets: the money market, the bond market, the equity market and the banking market. The detailed rules of its determination are presented by Bukowki (see Bukowski, 2020, pp. 56–57).

The quantity-based financial integration composite indicator is designed similarly to the price-based financial integration composite indicator. They are based on the indicators that describe the intra-Euro cross-border securities holdings expressed as a percentage of total securities holdings for the Euro area. The total is calculated as the sum of intra-Euro cross-border and domestic amounts. Three markets are taken into account: the interbank market, the bond market and the equity market (see Bukowski, 2020, p. 57).

The division criteria and types of financial integration indicators are listed in Table 3.1.

Table 3.1 The division criteria and types of financial integration indicators

Criterion of division	*Types of financial integration indicators*
After M. Pagano	• Indicators of credit and debt securities market integration • Indicators of share market integration • Integration indicators based on economic decisions of households and enterprises • Indicators of institutional differences
From the viewpoint of financial market segments	• Indicators of monetary market • Indicators of credit and deposit market • Indicators of treasury and corporate bond market • Indicators of share market
From the viewpoint of the design of integration indicators of financial markets	• Price-based and field-based indicators • News–based indicators • Quantity-based indicators
Synthetic indicators of financial market integration	• Price-based financial integration composite indicator • Quantity-based financial integration composite indicator

Source: The authors' own research on the basis of Pagano (2002), Bukowski (2011, 2020) and ECB (2005, 2021).

The above indicators are detailed in specialist literature (cf. Adam *et al.*, 2002; Baele *et al.*, 2004; ECB, 2005, 2021). The indicators to be applied to our research, whose results will be discussed in the part of this book concerning the integration of financial markets in the Euro area and the integration of the Polish financial market into financial markets of the Euro area, will be defined below. The choice of the indicators is determined by the availability of statistics about the Polish financial market that allow for a comparative analysis.

The price-based and field-based indicators include the measures of spread among the pricing of or returns on assets in the financial markets of various countries. The law of one price is the theoretical foundation of their design. They enable to test the degree to which the law is realised internationally. If some assets have the same or very similar characteristics, direct comparisons of prices or returns can be applied. Otherwise, the measures of this type must also reflect the impact of factors specific to markets in the particular countries, the differences of systemic risk levels and the degree of liquidity. The indicators of this group encompass the standard deviation of average interest on unsecured interbank loans, the standard deviation of average interest on bank deposits, standard deviation of average interest on bank credits, the spread between the rates of return (interest) on assets in a given market and those adopted as the benchmark, model of the spread for corporate bonds and the correlation of returns on stock indices.

The news-based indicators express the effect of information about anticipated shocks and the associated investment risk in financial markets. In fully integrated markets, investment portfolios should be well-diversified. Information coming from and concerning only local markets should have no major impact on the variations of asset pricing, as opposed to global information about an entire integrated market, which significantly affects price variations. The degree of systemic risk is the same in different countries whose markets are integrated. Thus, the indicators of this group show how far information specific to a local financial market is important to the remaining markets relative to the effect of global information. These indicators comprise the evolution of coefficient $\beta_{i,t}$, the impact of the growing effect of shared information component on the rate of return on shares.

The quantity-based indicators serve to assess the condition and progress of financial market integration. They are based on the volumes, values or shares of transactions among countries or regions. These indicators compliment the other measures of integration and include the ratio of international financial investments to total domestic financial assets, the ratio of capitalisation of foreign joint-stock companies to the total stock exchange capitalisation, the value of treasury bonds held by foreign entities to the total value of treasury bonds and the value of transborder transaction to total transactions.[1]

The synthetic indicators of financial market integration play a special role in the measurements of integration. They are detailed in the ECB report (2018) – *Financial Integration in Europe. Statistical Annex* and in S.I. Bukowski (2020, pp. 56–58).

The first of them is the "price-based financial integration composite indicator". It is constructed by a selection of price-based indicators concerning four main segments of financial markets: money market, bond market, equity market and banking market (see ECB, 2018, pp. 127–131). The first step in the process of constructing the "price-based financial integration composite indicator" is counting the indicators (sub-indices) which concern the above-mentioned segments. First, the indicators to be aggregated are homogenised by the application of a transformation which is based on an indicator's empirical cumulative distribution function (CDF). This function involves the computation of order statistics. The data are ranked in an ascending order for a time series of T observations of the indicator:

$$x = (x_1, x_2, \ldots, x_r),$$
$$\text{i.e. } x_{[1]} \le x_{[2]} \le \cdots \le x_{[T]}, \tag{3.1}$$

where $x_{[1]}$ represents the sample minimum (min(x)) and $x_{[T]}$ represents the sample maximum (max(x)).

The empirical CDF $F(x)$ which is equal to the number r of observations not exceeding a particular value x, divided by the total number T of observations in the sample, has the following form:

$$f(x) = \begin{cases} \frac{r}{T}, \mid for\, x_{[r]} \leq x < x_{[r+1]}, r = 1, 2, T-1 \\ 1, \mid for\, x \geq x_{[T]} \end{cases} \tag{3.2}$$

If the value for x occurs more than once, the ranking number assigned to each observation is set to the average for the ranks covered. The input series which are used for the composite indicator measure price dispersion. "Higher values of price dispersion tend to indicate a lower degree of financial integration. The transformation $1-F(x)$ is also applied in order to ensure that higher values of the indicator indicate a higher level of financial integration. After transformation, all input series are unit free and are, approximately, uniformly distributed within a range zero to one" (see ECB, 2018, p. 127).

The theoretical (ideal) benchmark value of zero is defined for all the dispersion measures of financial integration and a sample-dependent scaling factor is constructed as follows:

$$\theta^p(x) := \frac{\max(x) - \min(x)}{\max(x) - 0}, \tag{3.3}$$

where the superscript p differentiates the price-based scaling factor from that applied to the quantity-based financial integration composite indicator.

The price-based financial integration composite indicator has the following formula:

$$Z_t^p = \{1 - F(x_t)\}\theta^p(x) \tag{3.4}$$

All indicators concerning each of the market segments are aggregated into sub-indices

$$S_{i,t}^p = \frac{1}{N_i}\sum_{n=1}^{N_i} Z_{n,t}^p \tag{3.5}$$

for $i = 1,\ldots,4$.

The sub-indices are aggregated into the price-based financial integration composite indicator by computing weighted averages using size weights that reflect the relative size of the underlying financial market segment:

$$I_t^p = \sum_{i=1}^{4} w_i^p S_{i,t}^p \tag{3.6}$$

"The size weights are computed as the relative average amounts outstanding (taken from the aggregated Euro area financial accounts) for the base period 1997–2014, producing the following constant weights: money markets 17%, bond markets 36% and banking markets 32%" (see ECB, 2018, p. 127). Higher values of the indicator mean higher degrees of financial integration.

The second indicator is the "quantity-based financial integration composite indicator". This indicator is constructed similarly to the one presented above. They are based on the indicators which describe the intra-Euro cross-border securities holdings expressed as a percentage of total securities holdings for the Euro area. The total is calculated as the sum of intra-Euro cross-border and domestic amounts. The three markets are taken into account: interbank market (including the money market and banking market), bond market and equity market.

The "quantity-based financial integration composite indicator" is as follows:

$$I_t^Q = \sum_{i=1}^{3} w_i^Q S_{i,t}^Q \tag{3.7}$$

In the equation above, $S_{i,t}^Q$ represent the sub-indices referring to the three markets mentioned above; w_i^Q denotes the size weights which are computed as the relative average amounts outstanding, like in the case of the earlier described price-based indicators. The weights are as follows: in the case of the "*quantity-based financial integration composite indicator*": interbank markets 23%, bond markets 54% and equity markets 23% (see ECB, 2018, p. 131). The indices are constructed as follows:

$$S_{i,t}^Q = \frac{1}{N_i} \sum_{n=1}^{N_i} Z_{n,t}^Q \tag{3.8}$$

for $i = 1,\ldots,3$.

$Z_{n,t}^Q$ denote transformed and scaled indicators, defined as follows:

$$Z_t^Q = F(x_t)\theta^Q(x_t), \tag{3.9}$$

where $F(x_t)$ is CDF and $\theta^Q(x_t) := \dfrac{\max(x)}{BM_t}$ a time-varying scaling factor.

$$BM_t = \sum_{k=1}^{K} \omega_{k,t}\left(1 - \omega_{k,t}\right), \tag{3.10}$$

for t = 1,…,T.

A time varying benchmark which is computed for a given market segment with K countries; $\omega_{k,t}$ denotes a share of the total amount outstanding of a given asset class at a time t (see ECB, 2018, pp. 130–131).

Higher values of the "quantity-based financial integration composite indicator" mean higher degrees of financial integration.

The degree of financial market integration in the Euro area (synthetic measures)

A study of the degree of financial market integration was commissioned by the European Commission following the introduction of the single currency (Adam *et al.*, 2002, pp. 50–51). The measures of financial market integration served the purposes of the analysis. The research demonstrated that the interbank and sovereign debt markets were the best integrated. No integration applied to the credit market, evidenced with a low presence of foreign banks (with the exception of Ireland, Luxembourg and the United Kingdom). The share market's integration in the Euro area could be observed to grow, even though the measures examined did not always properly reflect the scale of this growth. The indicators of household decisions signalled a rising integration; yet, that was not corroborated in the case of enterprise mergers and takeovers. The legal regulations were highly varied, which might have had an adverse effect on the integration potential of financial markets. The study also showed that it was necessary to find new data in order to be better able to measure the financial market integration (see Adam *et al.*, 2002, pp. 50–51).

The degree of the financial market integration was also studied by the ECB (2015, 2018), Bukowski (2011, 2020) and Bukowski and Gowers (2016), among others.

The authors' assessment of the financial market integration concerns the Euro area in 1999–2020. Two measures are applied to the degree of financial market integration:

1 Price-based financial integration composite indicator.
2 Quantity-based financial integration composite indicator.

The quarterly and monthly financials in the European Central Bank (ECB) database are used.

The study proves that the degree of financial market integration gradually rose from the establishment of the Euro area to January 2006. The growth became a quantum leap in 2003–2006 (cf. Figure 3.1). The time of the financial and fiscal crisis in 2008–2012 was marked by a market fragmentation and a dramatic decline in the degree of financial market integration (see Figures 3.1 and 3.2).

This affected the share and treasury bond markets the most (Bukowski, 2020, pp. 88–91). As far as the specificity of the financial markets in the Euro area is concerned, the characteristics of the bank-oriented economy prevail. The bond sub-indices (chiefly of treasury bonds) and bank market sub-indices dominate the synthetic indicators of integration described in

Figure 3.1 Price-based financial integration composite indicator 1999–2020 (monthly data).

Source: The authors' own study based on the Financial Integration Indicators, Retrieved from www.ecb.europa.eu/stats/financial_markets_and_interest_rates/financial_integration/html/index.en.html on May 15, 2021.

the foregoing subsection, due to the bank orientation of the financial sector. Hence, the synthetic indicators reflect these characteristics. The financial and fiscal crisis in the Euro area, like the later crisis connected with the COVID-19 pandemic, above all gave rise to a fragmentation of the bond and banking (deposit and credit) markets.

Figure 3.2 Quantity-based financial integration composite indicator 1999–2020 (quarterly data).

Source: The authors' own study based on the Financial Integration Indicators, Retrieved from www.ecb.europa.eu/stats/financial_markets_and_interest_rates/financial_integration/html/index.en.html on May 15, 2021.

The situation began improving in 2012 and the degree of integration resumed its growth (cf. Figures 3.1 and 3.2). The policy of quantitative easing of the ECB has a substantial positive effect on the progress of the financial market integration. The research into the relationship between the policy of quantitative easing and the variations of the financial market integration in the Euro area in 2008–2016 by S. Bukowski (2020, p. 95) on the basis of two econometric models (one estimated by means of GLS Cochrane-Orcutt and the VAR model) suggests that the policy of quantitative easing had a significant impact on the increase in the degree of financial market integration. It was slowed beginning in 2020, however, by the COVID-19 pandemic crisis and the lockdowns in the Euro area countries. Again, the bond and banking (deposit and credit) markets were those most severely affected. It's to be expected that the gradual exit from the pandemic and lockdowns in the Euro area economies will cause the degree of financial market integration to rise.

Conclusion

The above analysis implies that the processes of financial market integration on an international scale are extraordinarily complex. They also encounter a range of major barriers. However, a broadly defined economic integration, including its financial, monetary and fiscal aspects, helps to reduce these barriers in the medium to long term.

A synthetic analysis of the changes of financial market integration in the Euro area provides the background for analysing the integration of insurance markets and for some comparisons with the other segments of the financial market, showing how unique a time it is for the economy and financial markets of the Euro area following the financial and fiscal crisis and another economic turmoil caused by the COVID-19 pandemic. The degree of integration of financial markets, including the monetary, deposit and credit (banking), share and treasury bond capital markets, began to rise after 2012. The pandemic-related economic crisis starting in 2020 has slowed the integration processes in financial markets, even reducing it when measured with synthetic indicators. A lot depends now on the surmounting of the effects of the economic crisis brought about by the COVID-19 pandemic. In the short and even the medium run, a continuing quantitative easing in the monetary policy and fiscal packages are bound to help the economy recover from the crisis and possibly enter the path to growth. It should be remembered, though, that an excessive money creation and budget deficits, as well as the associated rise of public debt, will generate negative long-term effects and another financial and fiscal crisis in the next ten years. This will most likely go hand in hand with a dynamic rise in inflation. The latter will largely be a result of the monetisation of budget deficits in some countries, on the one hand, and of expanding inflationary expectations triggered by rising budget deficits and public debt, on the other hand. These developments will unfortunately cause the fragmentation of financial markets to increase again and thus their integration to decline.

Note

1. See more about the design of financial market integration indicators in Bukowski (2020, pp. 47–56).

Bibliography

Adam, K., Japelli, T., Menichini, T., Padula, A. & Pagano, M., 2002. *Analyse, Compare, and Apply Alternative Indicators and Monitoring Methodologies to Measure the Evolution of Capital Market Integration in the European Union.*

Allen, F., Carletti, E., Qian, J. & Valenzuela, P., 2013. Does finance accelerate or retard growth? Theory and evidence. *Global Citizen Foundation Working Papers*, 4, pp. 5–24.

Baele, L., Ferrando, A., Hördal, P., Krylova, E. & Monnet, C., 2004. Measuring Financial Integration in the Euro Area. European Central Bank: Occasional Paper Series, No. 14/April.

Bednarski, P. & Polk, B., 2019. Should supervisors allow capital waivers to be used within European cross-border banking groups?. *Safe Bank*, 4 (77), pp. 23–49. doi: 10.26354/bb.2.4.77.2019.

Bekaert, G., Harvey, C. R. & Lumsdaine, R. L., 1998. *Dating the Integration of World Equity Markets.* Working Paper, No. 6724, Cambridge: NBER.

Biegun, K., 2015. Integracja rynków finansowych Polski i strefy Euro. *Studia Ekonomiczne. Zeszyty Naukowe Uniwersytetu Ekonomicznego w Katowicach*, 228, pp. 115–127.

Bukowski, S. I., 2020. *Financial Integration in the European Monetary Union.* London; New York: Routledge, Taylor & Francis Group.

Bukowski, S. I. & Gowers, R., 2016. The degree of integration of equity markets in Central Europe (New member EU countries) with the US and UK equity markets. *Central European Review of Economics & Finance*, 11 (1), pp. 5–26.

Bukowski, S. I., 2011. *Międzynarodowa integracja rynków finansowych.* Warszawa: Difin.

ECB, 2005. *Indicators of financial integration in the euro area.* Retrieved from https://www.ecb.europa.eu/stats/financial_markets_and_interest_rates/financial_integration/html/index.en.html on May 15, 2021.

ECB, 2015. *Domestic and cross-border positions of euro area monetary financial institutions, excluding the Eurosystem: Q2.* Retrieved from https://www.ecb.europa.eu/stats/money/aggregates/cross/html/domestic_cross_border_2015-04.en.html on October 14, 2015.

ECB, 2018. *Financial Integration in Europe. Statistical Annex.* Frankfurt am Main: European Central Bank. Retrieved from https://www.ecb.europa.eu/pub/pdf/fie/ecb.financialintegrationineurope201805.en.pdf on June 20, 2020.

ECB, 2021. *Indicators of financial integration in the euro area.* Retrieved from https://www.ecb.europa.eu/stats/financial_markets_and_interest_rates/financial_integration/html/index.en.html on May 15, 2021.

Guiso, L., Jappelli, T., Padula, M. & Pagano, M., 2004. *Financial Market Integration and Economic Growth in the EU.* Working Paper, No. 118, Salerno: University of Salerno, Centre for Studies in Economics and Finance.

London Economics, 2002. *Quantification of the Macro-Economic Impact of Integration of EU Financial Markets. Executive Summary.* Report to The European Commission – Directorate-General for the Internal Market, London Economics (in association with PricewaterhouseCoopers and Oxford Economic Forecasting), November 2002.

Pagano, M., 2002. *Measuring Financial Integration.* Frankfurt: European Central Bank.

Stirbu, C., 2004. *Financial Market Integration in a Wider European Union.* Discussion Paper, No. 297, Hamburg: Hamburg Institute of International Economics (HWWA).

Szypulewska-Porczyńska, A., 2017. Integracja rynków finansowych w strefie EURO – stan i perspektywy. *Prace Naukowe Uniwersytetu Ekonomicznego we Wrocławiu*, 466, pp. 193–202. doi: 10.15611/pn.2017.466.20

Thirlwall, A. P., 2006. *Growth & Development. With Special Reference to Developing Economies*, Basingstoke, New York: Palgrave, Macmillan.

Zabielski, K., 1999. *Finanse międzynarodowe.* Warszawa: Wydawnictwo Naukowe PWN.

4 The definitions, measures, barriers and effects of insurance market integration on an international scale

The integration of the insurance market on an international scale – Is it there?

The international integration of financial markets is already highly advanced both on a global, regional scale and, in particular, in the Euro area. Trade liberalisation, the liberalisation of the flow of manufacturing factors, including capital flows, and growing internationalisation, Information and Communication Technologies (ICT) progress and knowledge-based economy are at the heart of the said integration.

We have relatively good definitions, mechanism, indicators and know-how to analyse financial markets integration. Generally, though, we concentrate on the following segments: money markets, credit and deposit markets, and capital markets (stock and bond markets). Nobody deals with the insurance market integration. Of course, from the legal point of view, the European Union (EU) has regulations common to all the member countries (for example, one licence principle, Solvency II, etc.); yet from the economic and financial points of view, no up-to-date concept of that integration and its measures has been proposed.

Research into the single insurance market has been carried out by, among others, Giantsios and Noulas (2020, pp. 65–91), Cummnins and Rubrio-Misas (2018, pp. 1–49), Schoenmaker and Sass (2016, pp. 1–27), Kozarević *et al.* (2013, pp. 9–23), Njegomir and Marović (2012, pp. 134–142), Andelić *et al.* (2010, pp. 95–112) and Jurkiewicz and Wycinka (2006, pp. 277–290). It concerned the impact of integration on the development of insurance markets (Andelić *et al.*, 2010; Njegomir and Marović, 2012), the effectiveness of insurance companies (Cummnins and Rubrio-Misas, 2018; Giantsios and Noulas, 2020) and the insurance market internationalisation (Schoenmaker and Sass, 2016). The degree of insurance market integration is examined by Jurkiewicz and Wycinka (2006) and Kozarević *et al.* (2013). However, they propose no measures to assess the degree of integration of insurance markets.

The aim of this chapter is to answer the following question: what are the mechanism of insurance market integration and its measures?

DOI: 10.4324/9781003227762-4

Our hypothesis is as follows: the integration of insurance markets exists and we can find a proper measure of the degree of that integration.

In search of answers to the research question and in order to verify the research hypothesis, the literature on the subject and statistical data of insurance markets are reviewed.

The specificity of financial instruments is an important criterion of distinguishing the financial market segments. One of the legitimate and interesting divisions is W. Dębski's (see Dębski, 2003, p. 19). In his opinion, financial markets include the money market (financial instruments: interbank deposits, T-bills, commercial papers, bills, certificates of deposits, repo and reverse repo contracts), deposits and credit market (financial instruments: bank deposits, bank credits and loans), capital market (financial instruments: stocks, corporate bonds, treasury bonds, municipal bonds, investment certificates and depository receipts), derivatives market (financial instruments: forwards, financial futures, options and swaps) and foreign exchange market (financial instruments: currencies).

We can add one more insurance market (instruments – different products as policies concern different risks, but also abroad spectrum of life insurance policies with equity funds, etc.) to that classification. It is a unique market, at present partially associated with banking as bank assurance services. The insurance sector belongs to some important segments of the financial market. This is evidenced by both the share of insurance companies in the total number of financial institutions (Table 4.1) and the value of its assets in the total value of financial assets (Table 4.2).

The international integration of financial markets plays an important role in the development of financial markets and their impact on economic growth. Equity market integration on an international scale can be defined more precisely according to the law of one price. The application of this law means that assets generating identical monetary flows have the same price (rate of return and yield). In the case of shares, the price of capital raised in the financial market by issuing shares in two countries (regions) should be the same (see Adam et al., 2002, p. 4). However, in light of this definition, research concerning the process of financial markets integration on an international scale would be narrowed to unified issuance and listing rules for financial instruments. On an international scale, there are many exceptions to the law of single price, for example, due to restrictions that exempt some financial instruments in certain countries. Therefore, Baele *et al.* (see 2004, pp. 6–8) have formulated a broader definition of the integrated financial markets on an international scale: "the market for a given set of financial instruments and/or services is fully integrated if all potential market participants with the same relevant characteristics (1) face a single set of rules when they decide to deal in those financial instruments and/or services; (2) have equal access to the above-mentioned set of financial instruments and/or services; and (3) are treated equally when they are active in the market". Such a broad approach to the financial markets integration

Table 4.1 The share of insurance companies in the total number of financial institutions in 2004–2018

Specification	*2004*	*2005*	*2006*	*2007*	*2008*	*2009*	*2010*	*2011*	*2012*	*2013*	*2014*	*2015*	*2016*	*2017*	*2018*
Number of financial institutions	10,694	10,462	10,119	10,071	10,746	10,192	9921	9587	9076	8746	8362	8118	7601	7217	6949
Number of insurance companies	3769	3721	3602	3571	3558	3499	3431	3477	3373	3626	3250	3185	2609	2392	2200
Share of insurance companies in total number of financial institutions (%)	35.2	35.5	35.6	35.4	33.1	34.3	34.6	36.2	37.1	41.4	38.9	39.2	34.3	33.1	31.7

Source: The authors' own elaboration based on the European Central Bank (2020) and Insurance Data. Insurance Europe (2020).

Table 4.2 Structure of total global financial assets in 2018

Specification	*Total*	*Central banks*	*Banks*	*Public financial institutions*	*Insurance companies*	*Pensions found*	*Investments found*	*Others*
Value (USD trillion)	378.9	30.1	147.9	17.3	32.9	35.6	114.3	1.0
Share of total global financial assets (%)	100.0	7.9	39.0	4.6	8.7	9.4	30.2	0.3

Source: Financial Stability Board (2019).

also implies the law of one price. The law of one price causes assets to be characterised by identical risks and yields. The quoted definition comprises the law of one price. If the law of one price is not met, then there is room for arbitration which restores the law's validity (on condition, there are no barriers to the financial markets integration). In this context, it is not easy to adopt the definition to the international insurance markets (Bukowski, 2020, pp. 24–25).

Integrated insurance markets promote both competition and efficiency. One of the stages of integration were the Third Generation Directives (Council Directive 92/49/EEC of 18 June 1992 and Council Directive 92/96/EEC of 10 November 1992), which introduced a single EU licence whereby an insurer licenced in one EU country can do business in all EU countries without obtaining additional licences or being subject to regulations by host countries. The Directives also abolished substantive insurance supervision, freeing insurers from the regulation of prices and conditions as well as removing other regulatory impediments to competition. However, legal systems and institutional and cultural characteristics still differ significantly across EU countries (Cummins and Venard, 2008, pp. 295–326; Bikker and Gorter, 2011, pp. 163–184; Berry-Stölzle *et al.*, 2013, pp. 423–459; Cummins *et al.*, 2017, pp. 66–78; Bukowski and Lament, 2020, pp. 206–219).

The insurance market is characterised by certain specificities which make it difficult to assess integration processes. Therefore, the issues related to the integration of the insurance market constitute a poorly recognised research area. According to the basic concept of financial markets integration, the law of one price is in force. This means that in integrated financial markets, assets generating identical cash flows have the same price (rate of return). Referring it directly to the insurance market, it would mean that policyholders should be able to purchase insurance cover in each country (region) on the same conditions, regardless of the location of an insurance company. It can be assumed that if there are uniform legal regulations for conducting insurance activities, it is possible. Moreover, it is the subject of numerous legal analyses, which means that the phenomenon of integration of the insurance market in its legal aspect is both the subject of regulation in the adaptation of national regulations to supranational regulations, and scientific and research analyses. From the financial point of view, it is important to analyse it in the real sphere and demonstrate that such processes take place, and to examine the degree of this integration. It is not an easy question to study. While, for example, in the banking sector it is possible to analyse the interest rate on individual types of loans or the interest rate on deposits, in the insurance sector, one cannot directly compare the price of insurance protection (insurance premium) for individual types of insurance, or the value of claims and benefits from individual types of insurance. This is due to the differentiation of risk even within individual types of insurance and different insurance conditions. This means that the insurance premium (the price of the insurance cover) varies depending on the scope of the cover. Therefore, there is a problem with a thorough analysis and unambiguous comparison of insurance offers. The diversified scope of insurance coverage generates different prices that are difficult to compare unequivocally even within one national market for a given type of insurance. Hence, it is difficult to say whether there is a single price in the insurance market, and therefore the possibility of assessing the degree of integration of the insurance market.

The analysis shows that the insurance market, due to its specificity, is difficult to assess in terms of its integration. This does not mean, however, that no attempts have been made. Research into the integration of the insurance market has been carried out by, among others:

- Giantsios and Noulas (2020, pp. 65–91) – The authors estimated revenue efficiency and efficiency convergence with dynamic panel data models for 22 EU insurance markets during the financial crisis and after – in 2006–2014. In estimating the level of convergence, the concepts of β-convergence and σ-convergence are used. The results show that the average revenue efficiency is found to be relatively stable over the period 2006–2014 with a noticeable reduction for the period 2006–2008 due to the global financial crisis.
- Cummnins and Rubrio-Misas (2018, pp. 1–49) examine the impact of integration on the efficiency of EU life insurance markets in 1998–2011. The authors use Data Envelopment Analysis (DEA) and panel data models. In order to determine if the EU deregulation policies have succeeded in improving the efficiency and performance of life insurance sectors, the authors evaluate the dynamics of efficiencies obtained by DEA, a non-parametric frontier approach. In the analysis, efficiency is measured by comparing firms to "best practice" efficient frontiers formed by the most efficient firms in the industry. Financial market development, legal and governmental systems, as well as competitive intensity are found to affect insurance market performance and integration.
- Schoenmaker and Sass (2016, pp. 1–27) analyse the internationalisation of insurance groups and identify some scope for supervision connected with problems due to internationalisation. The empirical

findings suggest a high degree of cross-border penetration in European insurance. This high and increasing degree of internationalisation of European insurance groups poses a challenge for supervision – it may tilt the supervisory balance.

- Kozarević *et al.* (2013, pp. 9–23) research the process of integration of Western Balkan countries (Albania, Bosnia and Herzegovina, Croatia, Montenegro, Former Yugoslav Republic of Macedonia, Kosovo and Serbia) into the EU in 2002–2011. The Spearman's coefficient of rank correlation is used as the measurement of correlation in the development of the integration into the EU. The authors use the following indicators of insurance market development: total premium per capita, ratio of total premium to *Gross Domestic Product* (GDP), share of life insurance products, legal and institutional environment and solvency standard. The authors conclude that there is a strong positive correlation between the insurance development in the Western Balkan states and the process of their European integration.
- Njegomir and Marović (2012, pp. 134–142) have identified five key trends in the insurance market. These affect the insurance industry and the activity of insurance companies. They are integration processes, which encompass globalisation, consolidation and convergence, intensified catastrophic events and new risks, mainly caused by the emerging technologies. Integration is one of the factors which influences insurance market development.
- Andelić *et al.* (2010, pp. 95–112) analyse the influence of globalisation on the insurance and reinsurance markets of Eastern Europe from 2000 to 2008. The results confirm the significance of the relationship between globalisation trends and changes in the insurance and reinsurance markets of Eastern Europe. Integration is one of the factors which influences insurance market development.
- Jurkiewicz and Wycinka (2006, pp. 277–290) evaluate the level of European markets integration in 1999 by using multivariate statistical methods (Pearson correlation index, *k*-mean clustering, factor analysis and self-organising map). The authors use two groups of variables. The first group show the importance of insurance markets to the economy (premium/GDP, investment/GDP, investments in shares/market capitalisation, insurance employment/service, premium per inhabitant and insurance employment per inhabitant). The other group of variables describe the structure of insurance markets (provisions/premium ratio, number of companies per thousand inhabitants, share of the five largest life insurance companies, share of the five largest non-life insurance companies, share of life premium in total premium, share of life investment in total insurance investments, life investments/life premium, non-life investments/non-life premium and share of motor premium in total premium). According to the authors, the European insurance market is integrated on a very low level.

The analysis of the literature on the subject shows that the research so far has not in principle assessed the degree of integration of insurance markets. The integration of insurance markets was studied mainly as one of the factors of market development and improvement of their efficiency. Two studies – Jurkiewicz and Wycinka (2006) and Kozarević *et al.* (2013) – concern the assessment of the degree of integration of insurance markets; however, the proposed research methodology does not constitute a comprehensive approach, but only covers selected elements.

Definitions – Main problems and compromises

The price-based and field-based indicators include the measures of the spread between prices of or rates of return on assets in the financial markets of different countries. The theoretical basis of the construction of these indicators is the law of one price. They allow us to test the degree to which this law is applicable internationally. If assets have the same or similar characteristics, then it can be directly applied to compare prices or rates of return. Otherwise, the measures of this type have to also reflect the impact of specific factors related to the markets in particular countries, differences in the systemic risk level and liquidity level. The indicators of this type include the standard deviation of average interest on unsecured interbank loans, standard deviation of average interest on bank deposits, standard deviation of average interest on bank credits, spread between rates of return (interest rates) on assets in a given market and assets adopted as a benchmark, a spread model for corporate bonds and correlation of rates of return on equity market indexes (Bukowski, 2020, pp. 46–50).

News-based indicators recognise the impact of news concerning predicted shocks in financial markets and the related investment risk. In fully integrated markets, investment portfolios should be well-diversified. The information coming from local markets related exclusively to them should not have a significant effect on changes in asset prices, unlike global information related to the entire integrated market which affects price changes significantly. The systemic risk degree is the same in different countries whose markets have been integrated. Thus, the indicators of this group show how far the information specific to a local financial market is significant for the remaining markets in relation to the impact of information of a global character. These indicators include the evolution of coefficient $\beta_{i,t}$, the impact of the growing effect of the common news component on the rate of return on stocks.

The quantity-based indicators are used to assess the condition and course of financial markets integration. Their design is based on the data regarding the volume, value and share of transactions between countries and regions. They are indicators supplementing other measures of integration. They include, among others, the ratio of international financial investments to total domestic financial assets, the ratio of foreign joint stock companies capitalisation in a given equity market in relation to total equity market capitalisation, the ratio of the value of treasury bonds held by foreign entities to the total value of treasury bonds and the ratio of the cross-border transactions value to the total transactions value (Bukowski, 2020, pp. 46–50).

The problem is, however, that those measures cannot be simply applied to insurance market integration. Can we take the law of single price as a base for the construction of the measures of degrees of insurance market integration? It is a very important question. At first glance, it seems that we cannot. In the case of the equity, bond and money markets, the situation is simple in comparison to the integration of insurance markets. Does a single insurance premium exist in the EU or in the Euro area? No. Is the insurance premium a price like the price of bond or equity or is it an interest rate?

Our hypothesis is as follows: the integration of insurance markets takes place and we can find a proper measure of the degree of that integration.

The research covers the markets of the EU. The global insurance market can be divided into several regional markets. The most important markets in terms of the global market share measured by the insurance premium are EU-15, the United States and Advanced Asia-Pacific (Japan, South Korea, Taiwan, Australia, Hong Kong, Singapore and New Zealand). The structure of the global market and the characteristics of the above-mentioned segments are presented in Table 4.3.

The analysis of the data included in Table 4.3 shows that the EU-15 insurance market belongs to the significant segments of the global insurance market (a global market share of around 30%). Its development, measured with the insurance penetration and the insurance density rates, can be assessed as similar to the other two main segments of the global insurance market, though slightly weaker. The EU market can therefore be an appropriate research sample, the results for which can be treated as appropriate for the global insurance market.

An important limitation of the method is its theoretical nature. It is a proposed measure of the integration of insurance markets.

The measures of insurance market integration in the EU – Strengths and weaknesses

What is the definition? What are the main points of insurance market development which can be common? What are the premises of integration? What can be its indicators?

There are many problems for discussion:

The law of single price as a base for the measure of integration degree. Can we rely on the tendency of different insurance premiums (motor insurance,

Table 4.3 The main parts of the world insurance market in 1996–2018

	Premium volume (in billions of USD)			*Share of the world market (in %)*			*Insurance penetration rate: premium as a % of GDP*			*Insurance density rate: premiums per capita in USD*		
Specification	*1996*	*2008*	*2018*	*1996*	*2008*	*2018*	*1996*	*2008*	*2018*	*1996*	*2008*	*2018*
World	2106	4269	5193	100.0	100.0	100.0	7.3	7.1	6.1	431	634	682
EU-15	618	1564	1560	29.4	36.6	30.1	6.9	8.7	7.6	1611	3727	3276
United States	689	1346	1469	32.7	31.5	28.3	8.4	8.5	7.1	2333	3989	4481
Advanced Asia-Pacific[1]	520	675	927	24.7	15.8	17.1	11.7	10.4	9.7	4132	3173	3603

Source: The authors' own elaboration based on SwissRe data (SwissRe, 1998, 2008, 2019).

life insurance, etc.) to become increasingly closer? In the equity and bond markets, we have a differentiation of risk; in particular markets, the investment risk is different – is it the case for the different insurance markets, too? Maybe insurance premium can be good? How to measure the integration of a sub-segment of life insurance with capital funds? Is it possible to compare the usual life insurance premium in different countries of EU or Euro area?

We assume that a higher integration degree of country *i's* insurance market into foreign markets means a higher share of the written premium from insurance for foreign residents abroad in the total written premium of the home companies in country *i*.

To begin with, we propose the following approach. We assume that one of the main indicators in the field of insurance is the written premium. We treat that indicator as a base for the construction of the insurance market integration indicators.

Let's look at the main variables:

$WP_{hi,t}$ – *total written premium of home companies from the insurance for home residents, i country in period t.*

$WP_{fi,t}$ – *total written premium of home companies from insurance for foreign residents abroad in the region (home company directly), i country in period t.*

$WP^{L}_{hi,t}$ – *written premium from the insurance for home residents – life insurance, i country in period t – life insurance.*

$WP^{P}_{hi,t}$ – *written premium from the insurance for home residents – property insurance, i country in period t – non-insurance.*

$WP^{L}_{fi,t}$ – *written premium of home company from insurance for foreign residents abroad (home company directly), i country in period t – life insurance.*

$WP^{P}_{fi,t}$ – *written premium of home company from insurance for foreign residents abroad (home company directly), i country in period t – non-insurance.*

$W^{T}_{hfi,t}$ – *total written premium of home companies from the insurance for home residents and for foreign residents, i country in period t.*

$$WP_{hi,t} = WP^{L}_{hi,t} + WP^{P}_{hi,t} \tag{4.1}$$

$$WP_{fi,t} = WP^{L}_{fi,t} + WP^{P}_{fi,t} \tag{4.2}$$

$$W^{T}_{hi,t} = WP_{hi,t} + WP_{fi,t} \tag{4.3}$$

$$II_{i,t} = \frac{W_{fi,t}}{W^{T}_{hfi,t}} \tag{4.4}$$

A higher value of the indicator means a higher degree of country *i* integration into foreign insurance markets in the period *t*.

For all groups of countries:

$$II_g = \frac{\sum_{i=1}^{n} II_{i,t} d_{i,t}}{\sum_{i=1}^{n} d_{i,t}}, \tag{4.5}$$

$d_{i,t}$ – *number of inhabitants in country i in period t as the weight.*

A higher value of the indicator means a higher degree of integration of insurance market into the group of n countries (for example EU, the Euro area's countries) in the period t.

We also propose other indicators based on the concept of the quantity-based indicators.

$$Q_{i,t}^{P} = \frac{PI_{i,t}^{h} + PI_{i,t}^{f}}{GDP_{i,t}}, \tag{4.6}$$

where

$PI_{i,t}^{h}$ – the portfolio investment of the country *i's* insurance companies abroad in period t.
$PI_{i,t}^{f}$ – the portfolio investment of foreign insurance companies in country i in period t.
$GDP_{i,t}$ – GDP in country i in the period t.

A higher value of the indicator means a higher degree of country *i's* integration into foreign insurance markets in the period t.

For the group of countries:

$$Q_g = \frac{\sum_{i=1}^{n} Q_{i,t}^{P} d_{i,t}}{\sum_{i=1}^{n} d_{i,t}}, \tag{4.7}$$

$d_{i,t}$ – *number of inhabitants in country i in period t as the weight.*

A higher value of the indicator means a higher degree of integration of an insurance market into the group of n-countries (for example, the EU, the Euro area's countries) in the period t.

The proposed measures for assessing the degree of integration of insurance markets are based on the written premium and investments. The written premium is the income of an insurance company and the basis for many assessment indicators, as well as the price of insurance cover. It was divided into some groups of insurance market participants (home residents and foreign residents) and insurance products (life insurance and non-life insurance). The proposed indicator relates the premium written to the number of the population.

Investments of insurance companies have been included as the investment of a country's insurance companies abroad and the investment of foreign insurance companies in a country. They have been referenced to GDP. The proposed indicators refer to the insurance penetration rate and the insurance density rate. However, a different scope of the written premium is worth noting. In the proposed measure, it includes the premium in a broader sense – from home residents and foreign residents. The classic insurance density rate includes insurance companies operating in a given insurance market. The second proposed indicator relates investment to GDP. The classic insurance penetration rate compares the insurance premium to GDP. Thus, these are other indicators, covering both domestic and foreign insurance companies. This has not been included in the indicators so far. The proposed methodology for assessing the degree of integration of insurance markets is proprietary and has not yet been applied in practice. This is also indicated by the research conducted in the literature on the subject. The assessment of the degree of integration of insurance markets was the subject of research in two studies: Jurkiewicz and Wycinka (2006) and Kozarević *et al.* (2013). The first evaluated the level of European markets integration in one year. Fifteen indicators were used for the evaluation. The proposed methodology included various measures, which allowed to test a wider scope of integration. However, the authors themselves emphasised that the indicators correlated with each other, which resulted in the need to eliminate them. In the proposed set of indicators, they should rather not be correlated – the indicators capture different values: written premium, population, investments and GDP.

In the other study, Kozarević *et al.* (2013) researched the process of integration of Western Balkan countries into the EU. The authors used the following indicators of insurance market development: total premium per capita, ratio of total premium to GDP, share of life insurance products, legal and institutional environment, and solvency standard. The study made it possible to assess the impact of the above-mentioned indicators on the development of the surveyed insurance markets and compare them with the results for the EU insurance market. In principle, therefore, no index was proposed to assess the degree of integration of insurance markets.

Summing up, it should be stated that neither in the literature on the subject nor in insurance practice there is a measure assessing the degree of integration of insurance markets. Our proposal is innovative, but it is still at the theoretical stage. Conducting empirical research may contribute to the correction of the adopted assumptions.

Barriers to the insurance market integration in the EU

Like in the case of other financial markets, barriers connected with economic policy and the operation of economies and financial markets, with differences in the systems of trade and financial laws, with multiple currencies, and lack of harmonised settlements of financial transactions on an international scale can be distinguished in the process of insurance market integration on an international scale, too (see Bukowski, 2020, pp. 28–29). The first group of barriers comprises the effects of economic policy on capital flows, the effects of international fiscal policy differences on the financial sector, including insurance, the differences in the competitiveness of financial markets in the economies of particular countries, the variability of macroeconomic and insurance risks across countries and the asymmetries of information between foreign and domestic investors.

Restrictions to capital flows on an international scale, the regulations of capital pricing and those limiting free capital allocation on an international scale (e.g., restrictions on the structure of investment portfolio of insurance firms) adversely affect the integration processes of financial markets, including insurance. Excessive taxation, especially of assets of the financial sector firms, including the insurance sector, has negative impacts. The imperfect competitiveness of financial markets, including insurance, exhibited as excessive monopolisation, limitations to competition among insurance institutions and low transparency produce differences in capital costs and high prices of intermediary insurance companies. The diversification of macroeconomic risk across countries plays a major role in the integration processes of insurance markets, like of the other financial markets. Those differences influence the levels of risk premium, the required rates of return and consequently the direction and intensity of capital flows among countries (see Bukowski, 2020, p. 28). The macroeconomic risk is significantly related to the budget deficit and public debt in a given country. A rise in these macroeconomic quantities leads to a higher macroeconomic risk, which then adversely affects foreign investments.

As far as the second group of barriers is concerned, the negative effect needs to be stressed of significant differences in the legal systems governing the foundation and operation of insurance companies in particular countries on the processes of integration of insurance markets, like of the remaining financial markets. This relates, inter alia, to the rules of corporate functioning, of introducing financial instruments to public trade, and the standards of accounting. Some differences in the taxation systems of insurance companies may constitute barriers as well.

The asymmetry of information between foreign and domestic investors is another serious barrier. It arises from the imperfection of financial markets, the dispersion of information and the imperfection of its international flows. These factors are a cause of home bias, the investors' tendency to keep mainly domestic financial assets in their portfolios. This has a substantial effect on the composition of insurance firms' investment portfolios. The above factors may considerably impede capital flows.

The international multiplicity of currencies is one of the strongest barriers. The presence of many currencies is closely associated with the currency risk of foreign investments, both direct and portfolio. As the rates of exchange fluctuate, the uncertainty as to future capital pricing, the cost of exchange risk and protection against it escalate.

In the EU, a number of these barriers to the process of financial and insurance market integration have been largely overcome or alleviated through a harmonisation of the EU laws relating to the operating principles of the financial markets, banking and insurance sectors, and the standards of accounting. In addition, most EU countries are within the Euro area and are not affected by the border effect of the multiple currencies.[2]

The effects of international insurance market integration

The integration of insurance markets on an international scale affects the economic growth by stimulating the development of the insurance market as a part of the financial development (see Figure 4.1). The process of insurance market integration, like of other segments of the financial market, increases inflows of foreign capital to the insurance sector in a country, which improves the effectiveness of insurance companies.

The competition enhances, too, the cost of insurance services declines and the negative selection of those entering into contracts of insurance is reduced. The access of enterprises and households to the large international insurance market, the financial stability and security of insurance companies improve as the effect of risk sharing is applied to the formation of investment portfolios. The effectiveness of capital allocation improves. What is

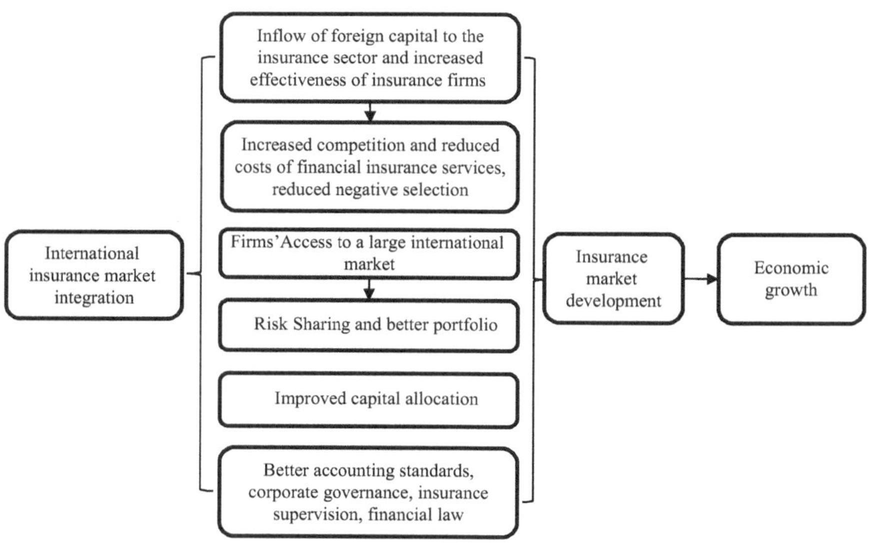

Figure 4.1 Theoretical correlation between international insurance market integration and financial development and economic growth.

Source: Bukowski (2011, p. 35).

more, the international integration of insurance markets (through the harmonisation of legal regulations) leads to the improvements of accounting standards, corporate governance, insurance supervision and the associated prudential rules, and financial law. In effect, the integration of financial markets helps improve the effectiveness of insurance companies and fosters economic growth.

Conclusion

We believe that the proposed indicators based on the written premium and mutual foreign investment between countries are very good introductory measures of insurance market integration in the EU and Euro area. It is a quantity-based indicator. Up to present, no indicators measuring the degree of insurance market integration have been suggested. Generally, if anybody has dealt with the problem of insurance market integration, they addressed legal problems and problems of regulations of insurance markets within the EU. We have been interested in the design of indicators which will be practically useful for the annual reports concerning the degree of insurance market integration. Our research will proceed to test the presented indicators using real statistical data.

An important limitation of the method is its theoretical nature. It is a proposed measure of the integration of insurance markets.

The insurance market integration on an international scale influences economic growth like it does the other financial markets like the stock exchange market, bond market, money market, and credit and deposit (banking) market. It affects the development of insurance market as a component of financial development. The latter influences economic growth.

Notes

1. Japan, South Korea, Taiwan, Australia, Hong Kong, Singapore and New Zealand.
2. Concerning the legal regulations of financial markets, cf. Bukowski (2020, pp. 61–68) and Chapter 1 of this book.

Bibliography

Adam, K., Japelli, T., Menichini, T., Padula, A. & Pagano, M., 2002. *Analyse, Compare, and Apply Alternative Indicators and Monitoring Methodologies to Measure the Evolution of Capital Market Integration in the European Union*. Basel: European Commission.

Andelić, G. B., Ćosić, I. & Daković, V., 2010. The impact of globalization on the insurance and reinsurance market of Eastern Europe. *South East European Journal of Economics and Business*, 4, pp. 95–112. doi.10.2478/v10033-010-0010-7.

Baele, L., Ferrando, A., Hördal, P., Krylova, E. & Monnet, C., 2004. Measuring financial integration in the Euro area. European Central Bank: Occasional Paper Series, 14.

Berry-Stölzle, T., Hoyt, R. E. & Wende, S., 2013. Capital market development, competition, property rights, and the value of insurer product-line diversification: A cross-country analysis. *Journal of Risk and Insurance*, 80 (2), pp. 423–459. doi.10.1111/j.1539-6975.2012.01470.x.

Bikker, J. A. & Gorter, J., 2011. Restructuring of the Dutch non-life insurance industry: Consolidation, organizational form and focus. *Journal of Risk and Insurance*, 78, pp. 164–184. doi.10.1111/j.1539-6975.2010.01369.x.

Bukowski, S. I., 2011. *Międzynarodowa integracja rynków finansowych*, Warszawa: Difin.

Bukowski, S. I., 2020. *Financial Integration in the European Monetary Union*. London; New York: Routledge, Taylor & Francis Group.

Bukowski, S. I. & Lament, M., 2020. Foreign capital impact on insurance market development in EU-15 countries. *Entrepreneurial Business and Economics Review*, 8 (3), pp. 206–219. doi. 10.15678/EBER.2020.080312.

Council Directive 92/49/EEC of 18 June 1992 on the coordination of laws, regulations and administrative provisions relating to direct insurance other than life assurance and amending Directives 73/239/EEC and 88/357/EEC (third non-life insurance Directive). Official Journal of the European Communities on 11.8.92, No. L 228/1.

Council Directive 92/96/EEC of 10 November 1992 on the coordination of laws, regulations and administrative provisions relating to direct life assurance and amending Directives 79/267/EEC and 90/619/EEC (third life assurance Directive). Official Journal of the European Communities on 9.12.92, No. L 360/1.

Cummins, J. D., Rubio-Misas, M. & Vencappa, D., 2017. Competition, efficiency and soundness in European life insurance markets. *Journal of Financial Stability*, 28, pp. 68–78. doi.10.1016/j.jfs.2016.11.007.

Cummins, J. D. & Venard, B., 2008. Insurance market dynamics: Between global developments and local contingencies. *Risk Management and Insurance Review*, 11 (2), pp. 295–326. doi. 10.1111/j.1540-6296.2008.00142.x.

Cummnins, J. D. & Rubrio-Misas, M., 2018. Integration and efficiency convergence in European life insurance markets. Retrieved from http://EFMA2018_0482_fullpaper.pdf on August 10, 2020.

Dębski, W., 2003. *Rynek finansowy i jego mechanizmy. Podstawy teorii i praktyki*. Warszawa: PWN.

European Central Bank, 2020. Statistical Data Warehouse. Retrieved from http://sdw.ecb.europe.eu on August 10, 2020.

Financial Stability Board, 2019. Global Monitoring Report on Non-Bank Financial Intermediation 2019. Retrieved from http://fsb.org/terms_conditions/ on August 10, 2020.

Giantsios, D. G. & Noulas, A. G., 2020. Efficiency and convergence in the European life insurance industry. *Multinational Finance Journal*, 24 (1/2), pp. 65–91.

Insurance Data. Insurance Europe, 2020. Retrieved from http://insuranceeurope.eu on August 15, 2020.

Jurkiewicz, T. & Wycinka, E., 2006. Evaluation of the degree of integration among European insurance markets. *Acta Universitatis Lodziensis. Folia Oeconomica*, 196, pp. 277–290.

Kozarević, S., Kozarević, E. & Šiljegović, E., 2013. Insurance market development in the context of integration to the European Union: A case of the Western Balkans. *International Journal of Economic Perspectives*, 7 (1), pp. 9–23.

Njegomir, V. & Marović, B., 2012. Contemporary trends in the global insurance industry. *Procedia – Social and Behavioral Sciences*, 44, pp. 134–142. doi: 10.1016/j.sbspro.2012.05.013.

Schoenmaker, D. & Sass, J., 2016. Cross-border insurance in Europe: Challenges for supervision. *The Geneva Papers on Risk and Insurance – Issues and Practice*, 41, pp. 1–27. doi.org/10.1057/gpp.2015.35.

SwissRe 1998. *World Insurance*, Sigma SwissRe 4/98.

SwissRe, 2008. *World Insurance*, Sigma SwissRe 3/2008.

SwissRe, 2019. *World Insurance*, Sigma SwissRe 43/2019.

5 Insurance market integration in the EU

The degree of insurance market integration in the EU and in the Euro area (1999–2019)

The degree of the insurance market integration in the European Union (EU) and in the Euro area is estimated on the basis of the formulas in Chapter 4. The data from OECD Statistics (2021), EIOPA Database (2021), Eurostat Database (2021), ORBIS Database (2021) and Insurance Europe (2021) (the figures concerning the insurance markets), AMECO Database (2021) and ECB Statistical Data Warehouse (2021) (macroeconomic and monetary data) databases are utilised. Unfortunately, the available data on the insurance market cover annual periods; therefore, the remaining macroeconomic and monetary data are obtained on an annual basis. Quarterly figures would be far better; of course, they are unavailable for insurance markets, however. What is more, those available data cover the period from 1999 to 2019.

In order to illustrate the extent of variables concerning insurance markets studied and their distribution in the time examined, the following tables and graphs contain some key statistics for those variables. They are analysed in respect of the EU and Euro area countries. The basic statistics characterising the variables in respect of gross written premium in the EU are presented in Table 5.1 and Figure 5.1.

A review of the data concerning the development of insurance premium in the EU countries in 1999–2019, included in Table 5.1 and Figure 5.1, shows their internal diversity. This is signalled by variance and standard deviation, which depict the dispersion around the average. Causes of the considerable dispersion in the distributions of the variables can be attributed to the large grouping of the countries studied, a high diversity of their insurance market development and the rather long period of research, which the basic statistics show to have been varied – hence the large differences between the minimum and maximum values of the variables.

Table 5.2 and Figure 5.2 show the key statistics on the investments by insurance companies active in the EU markets in 1999–2019.

DOI: 10.4324/9781003227762-5

Table 5.1 Basic statistics concerning the variables studied of the EU insurance markets in 1999–2019 – Gross written premium

Specification	*D in C (Total)*	*D in C (Life)*	*D in C (Non-life)*	*D in A (Total)*	*D in A (Life)*	*D in A (Non-life)*	*F in C (Total)*	*F in C (Life)*	*F in C (Non-life)*
N importance	588	588	588	588	588	588	588	588	588
Average	49,829.39	29,103.48	20,227.04	6435.03	3780.83	2654.03	1207.41	584.32	622.23
Median	8033.400	4674.100	3879.532	272.487	76.399	75.837	91.413	22.869	44.461
Maximum	64,4556.5	53,6103.9	23,1556.8	83,612.7	62,698.1	28,795.8	24,525.5	23,984.9	9109.7
Minimum	95.663	0.996	67.087	0.00000	0.00000	0.00000	0.00000	0.00000	0.00000
Variance	9.162295E+09	3.725148E+09	1.611446E+09	3.073116E+08	1.499917E+08	3.604603E+07	1.093421E+07	7.799037E+06	2.676875E+06
Standard deviation	95,719.88	61,033.9909	40,142.8241	17,530.3056	12,247.11	6003.83	3306.69	2792.68	1636.12

Source: The authors' own research based on STATISTICA 12.

Explanation: D in C (Total) – domestic gross written premium of domestic insurance companies (US Dollar, Million); D in C (Life) – domestic gross written premium of domestic life insurance companies (US Dollar, Million); D in C (Non-life) – domestic gross written premium of domestic non-life insurance companies (US Dollar, Million); D in A (Total) – gross written premium abroad of domestic insurance companies (US Dollar, Million); D in A (Life) – gross written premium abroad of domestic life insurance companies (US Dollar, Million); D in A (Non-life) – gross written premium abroad of domestic non-life insurance companies (US Dollar, Million); F in C (Total) – domestic gross written premium of foreign insurance companies (US Dollar, Million); F in C (Life) – domestic gross written premium of foreign life insurance companies (US Dollar, Million); F in C (Non-life) – domestic gross written premium of foreign non-life insurance companies (US Dollar, Million).

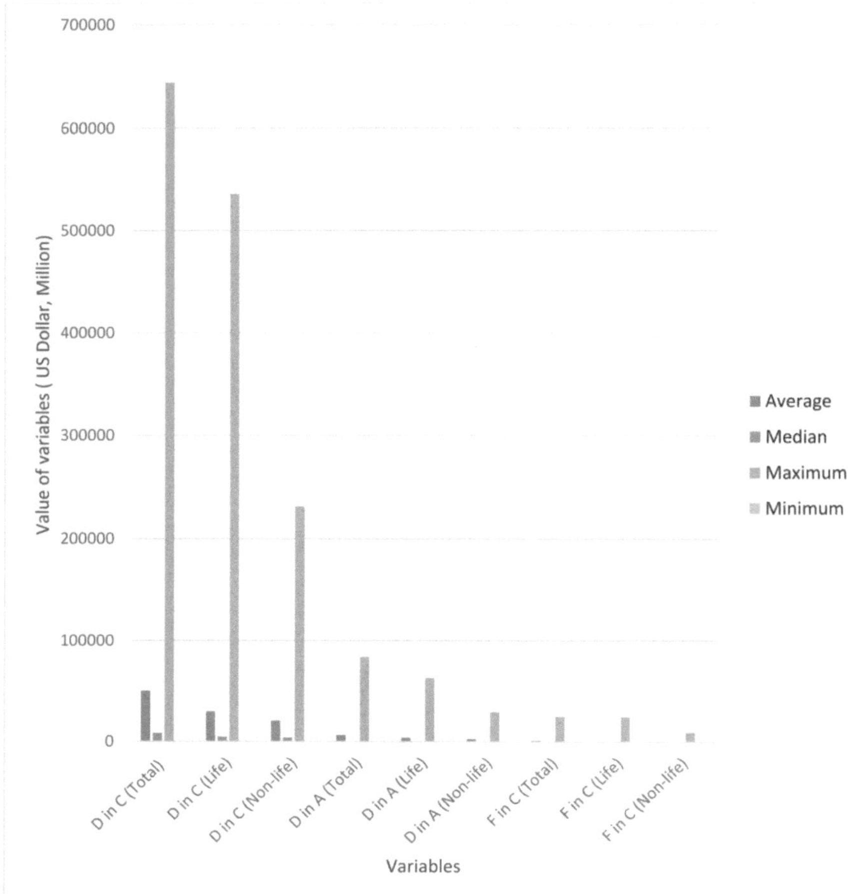

Figure 5.1 Selected basic statistics concerning the variables studied of the EU insurance markets in 1999–2019 – Gross written premium.

Source: The authors' own research.

Explanation: D in C (Total) – domestic gross written premium of domestic insurance companies (US Dollar, Million); D in C (Life) – domestic gross written premium of domestic life insurance companies (US Dollar, Million); D in C (Non-life) – domestic gross written premium of domestic non-life insurance companies (US Dollar, Million); D in A (Total) – gross written premium abroad of domestic insurance companies (US Dollar, Million); D in A (Life) – gross written premium abroad of domestic life insurance companies (US Dollar, Million); D in A (Non-life) – gross written premium abroad of domestic non-life insurance companies (US Dollar, Million); F in C (Total) – domestic gross written premium of foreign insurance companies (US Dollar, Million); F in C (Life) – domestic gross written premium of foreign life insurance companies (US Dollar, Million); F in C (Non-life) – domestic gross written premium of foreign non-life insurance companies (US Dollar, Million).

Table 5.2 Basic statistics concerning the variables studied of the EU insurance markets in 1999–2019 – Investments of insurance companies

Specification	*ID in A*	*IF in C*
N importance	588	588
Average	23,939.45	40,069.35
Median	684.129	6654.520
Maximum	385,128.8	387,523.7
Minimum	0.00	0.00
Variance	3.398797E+09	5.157382E+09
Standard deviation	58,299.20	71,814.92

Source: The authors' own research on STATISTICA 12.

Explanation: ID in A – investments of domestic insurance companies abroad (US Dollar, Million); IF in C – domestic investments of foreign insurance companies (US Dollar, Million).

An analysis of the data in Table 5.2 and Figure 5.2 shows that the variables for the investments of insurance companies active in the EU markets in 1999–2019 are internally diversified. This is affirmed by both the variables assessing the dispersion – variance and standard deviation, which demonstrate a significant dispersion of the variables around the average – and those estimating the maxima and minima, evidence of a large diversity of the variables' distribution. With reference to the premium, causes of the considerable dispersion in the distributions of the variables examined can be attributed to the large grouping of the countries studied, a high diversity of their insurance market development and the rather long period of research, which the basic statistics show to have been varied – hence the large differences between the minimum and maximum values of the variables.

Table 5.3 and Figure 5.3 show the key statistics regarding the variables concerning gross written premium in the Euro area countries in 1999–2019.

An analysis of the figures in Table 5.3 and Figure 5.3 proves that they are internally varied, although they relate to a more homogeneous group of objects – the Euro area countries. This is suggested by variance and standard deviation, which illustrate the dispersion around the average. The causes of the considerable dispersion in the distributions of the variables examined, like with reference to all the EU countries, can be traced to the large grouping of the countries studied (there are 19 in the Euro area), a high diversity of their insurance market development and the rather long period of research, which the basic statistics show to have been varied – hence the large differences between the minimum and maximum values of the variables.

Table 5.4 and Figure 5.4 show the key statistics on the investments by insurance companies active in the Euro area markets in 1999–2019.

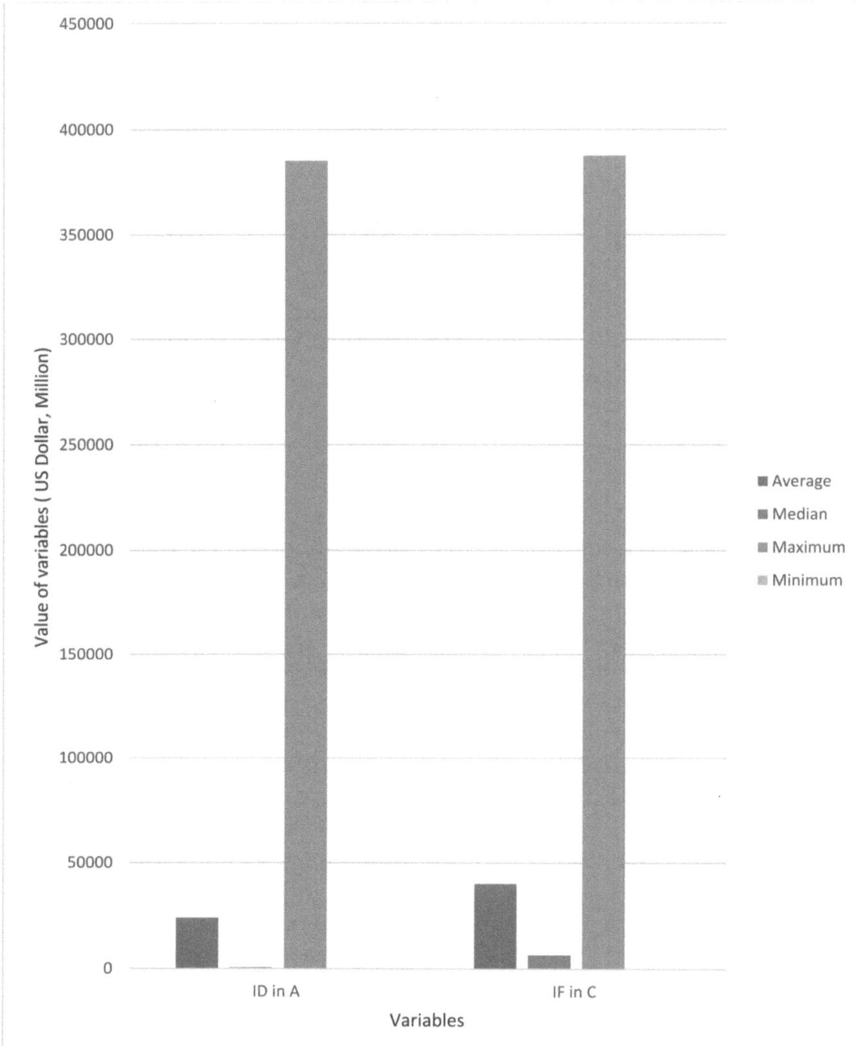

Figure 5.2 Selected basic statistics concerning the variables studied of the EU insurance markets in 1999–2019 – Investments of insurance companies.

Source: The authors' own research.

Explanation: ID in A – investments of domestic insurance companies abroad (US Dollar, Million); IF in C – domestic investments of foreign insurance companies (US Dollar, Million).

Table 5.3 Basic statistics concerning the variables studied of the Euro area countries' insurance markets in 1999–2019 – Gross written premium

Specification	*D in C (Total)*	*D in C (Life)*	*D in C (Non-life)*	*D in A (Total)*	*D in A (Life)*	*D in A (Non-life)*	*F in C (Total)*	*F in C (Life)*	*F in C (Non-life)*
N importance	399	399	399	399	399	399	399	399	399
Average	49,247.25	25,925.27	22,634.86	5699.76	3134.97	2564.54	1101.56	800.09	300.22
Median	12,117.87	6493.40	3970.32	355.54	200.31	185.46	129.33	34.10	71.48
Maximum	344,268.1	188,634.3	231,556.8	83,612.7	62,698.1	28,795.8	24,525.5	23,984.9	3691.1
Minimum	95.66300	0.99600	67.08700	0.00000	0.00000	0.00000	0.00000	0.00000	0.00000
Variance	6.948162E+09	1.820580E+09	1.892147E+09	2.405900E+08	1.178702E+08	3.274347E+07	1.224865E+07	1.128318E+07	4.466973E+05
Standard deviation	83,355.63	42,668.25	43,498.81	15,510.96	10,856.80	5722.19	3499.81	3359.04	668.35

Source: The authors' own research on the basis of STATISTICA 12.

Explanation: D in C (Total) – domestic gross written premium of domestic insurance companies (US Dollar, Million); D in C (Life) – domestic gross written premium of domestic life insurance companies (US Dollar, Million); D in C (Non-life) – domestic gross written premium of domestic non-life insurance companies (US Dollar, Million); D in A (Total) – gross written premium abroad of domestic insurance companies (US Dollar, Million); D in A (Life) – gross written premium abroad of domestic life insurance companies (US Dollar, Million); D in A (Non-life) – gross written premium abroad of domestic non-life insurance companies (US Dollar, Million); F in C (Total) – domestic gross written premium of foreign insurance companies (US Dollar, Million); F in C (Life) – domestic gross written premium of foreign life insurance companies (US Dollar, Million); F in C (Non-life) – domestic gross written premium of foreign non-life insurance companies (US Dollar, Million).

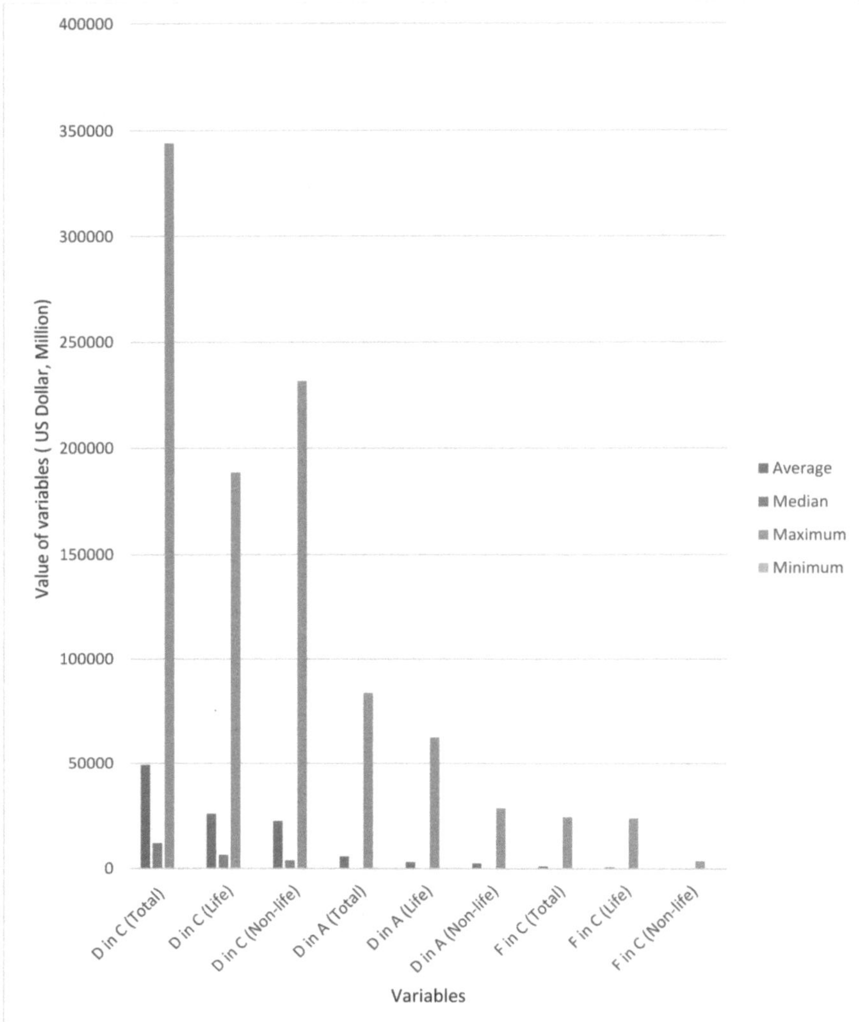

Figure 5.3 Selected basic statistics concerning the variables studied of the Euro area countries insurance markets in 1999–2019 – Gross written premium.

Source: The authors' own research.

Explanation: D in C (Total) – domestic gross written premium of domestic insurance companies (US Dollar, Million); D in C (Life) – domestic gross written premium of domestic life insurance companies (US Dollar, Million); D in C (Non-life) – domestic gross written premium of domestic non-life insurance companies (US Dollar, Million); D in A (Total) – gross written premium abroad of domestic insurance companies (US Dollar, Million); D in A (Life) – gross written premium abroad of domestic life insurance companies (US Dollar, Million); D in A (Non-life) – gross written premium abroad of domestic non-life insurance companies (US Dollar, Million); F in C (Total) – domestic gross written premium of foreign insurance companies (US Dollar, Million); F in C (Life) – domestic gross written premium of foreign life insurance companies (US Dollar, Million); F in C (Non-life) – domestic gross written premium of foreign non-life insurance companies (US Dollar, Million).

Table 5.4 Basic statistics concerning the variables studied of the Euro area countries insurance markets in 1999–2019 – The investments of insurance companies

Specification	*ID in A*	*IF in C*
N importance	399	399
Average	21,678.07	45,750.55
Median	908.664	6549.907
Maximum	324,473.0	387,523.7
Minimum	0.00	0.00
Variance	2.436796E+09	6.403314E+09
Standard deviation	49,363.92	80,020.71

Source: The authors' own research on the basis of STATISTICA 12.

Explanation: ID in A – investments of domestic insurance companies abroad (US Dollar, Million); IF in C – domestic investments of foreign insurance companies (US Dollar, Million).

An analysis of the figures in Table 5.4 and Figure 5.4 proves that they are internally varied, although they relate to a more homogeneous group of objects – the Euro area countries. This is affirmed by both the variables assessing the dispersion – variance and standard deviation, which demonstrate a significant dispersion of the variables around the average – and those estimating the maxima and minima, evidence of a large diversity of the variables' distribution.

The chapter continues with the results concerning the integration of the EU insurance markets in 1999–2019. The study covers the countries of the EU and of the Euro area. The degree of integration is measured with original measures of integration described in Chapter 4.

Figures 5.5 and 5.6 imply the integration of insurance markets in the EU countries measured by means of II_g declined in 1999–2006, to rise till 2012, and shrink again by 2014. The ratio grew in 2015, dropped a little in 2018 and increased in 2019 (see Figure 5.5).

An examination of the extent of integration of the EU insurance markets by means of Q_g, however, points to its nearly permanent growth in 1999–2019, with brief decline episodes in 2008 (the financial crisis) and at the turn of 2014/2015 (see Figure 5.6).

In the Euro area, the ratio of insurance market integration $\mathrm{II_g}$ is similar like in the whole EU as far as the drops and rises are concerned. The ratio is a little higher for the Euro area than in the EU (see Figure 5.7).

The ratio $\mathrm{Q_g}$ exhibits a marked difference. Its review shows a nearly uninterrupted growth in the degree of integration (see Figure 5.8).

All in all, a review of $\mathrm{II_g}$ and $\mathrm{Q_g}$ indicates a growing degree of insurance market integration both in the entire EU and in the Euro area in the period studied, in particular, in 2006–2019, where both the ratios demonstrate it.

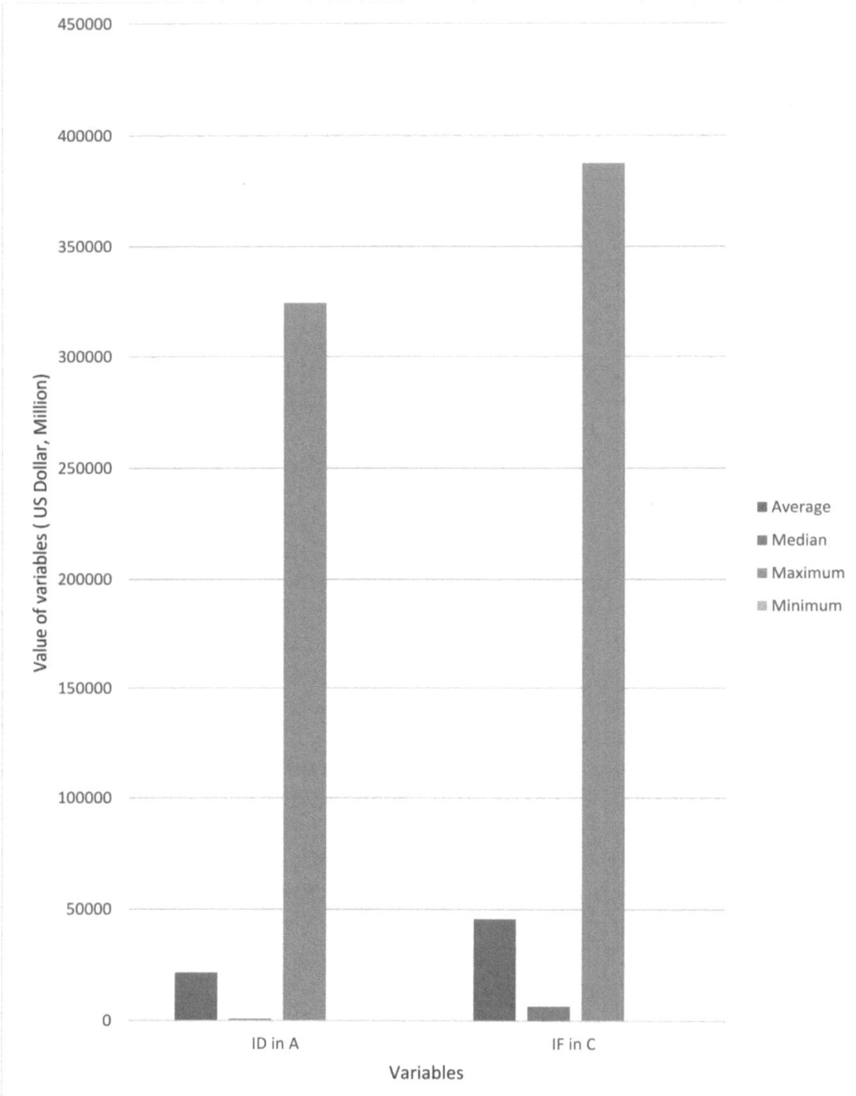

Figure 5.4 Selected basic statistics concerning the variables studied of the Euro area countries insurance markets in 1999–2019 – The investments of insurance companies.

Source: The authors' own research.

Explanation: ID in A – investments of domestic insurance companies abroad (US Dollar, Million); IF in C – domestic investments of foreign insurance companies (US Dollar, Million).

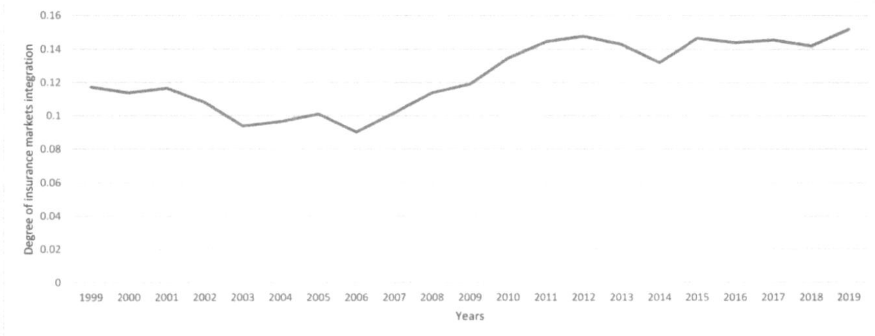

Figure 5.5 The degree of insurance market integration in the EU countries – II_g in 1999–2019.

Source: Own calculation based on the OECD Statistics and Insurance Europe.

Insurance market integration and economic growth in the EU and in the Euro area (1999–2019)

To determine the impact of the insurance market integration on economic growth in the EU and Euro area countries, the following model is constructed for both the cases:

$$lnGDP_t = a_0 + a_1 lnNCF_t + a_2 lnIIg_t + a_3 lnQg_t + u_t \quad (5.1)$$

where

GDP_t – gross domestic product in the EU and Euro area, respectively, in constant price terms (2010)
NCF_t – net capital formation as a proxy for investment in economies for the EU and Euro area, respectively, in constant price terms (2010)
IIg, Qg – the ratios of insurance market integration specified in Chapter 4
ln – natural logarithm
u_t – random factor

Annual data are applied. The model is built by means of backward stepwise regression.

The results of model estimation for the EU

Engle-Granger cointegration test suggests the cointegration of the time series utilised in the model (cf. the test results below).

Augmented Dickey-Fuller test for uhat testing down from 1 lags, criterion AIC
sample size 20, unit-root null hypothesis: a = 1,
test without constant including 0 lags of (1 – L)uhat

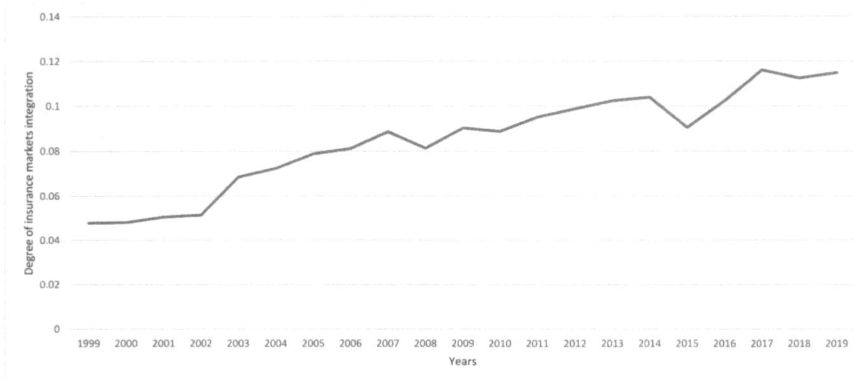

Figure 5.6 The degree of the EU insurance market integration measured with Q_g in 1999–2019.

Source: Own calculation based on the OECD Statistics and Insurance Europe.

model: (1 – L)y = (a – 1) × y(–1) + e
estimated value of (a – 1): –0.978803
test statistic: tau_ct(4) = –4.81141 with critical value equal –1.95 with a significance level 0.05
p-value 0.08865, 1st-order autocorrelation coeff. for e: –0.014.

The results in Table 5.5 show that all the variables are statistically significant, the normal distribution of the model's residuals applies and there is no ARCH effect, residue autocorrelation or heteroskedasticity.

The model explains 95% of the dependent variable's variance, which proves its good fit. The degree of insurance market integration, measured with II_g and Q_g, has a statistically significant effect on economic growth in the EU countries.

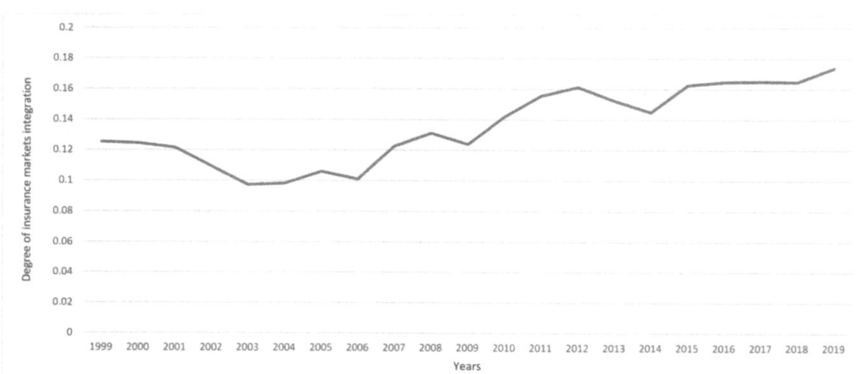

Figure 5.7 The degree of insurance market integration in the Euro area countries, measured with II_g, in 1999–2019.

Source: The authors' own calculation based on the OECD Statistics and Insurance Europe.

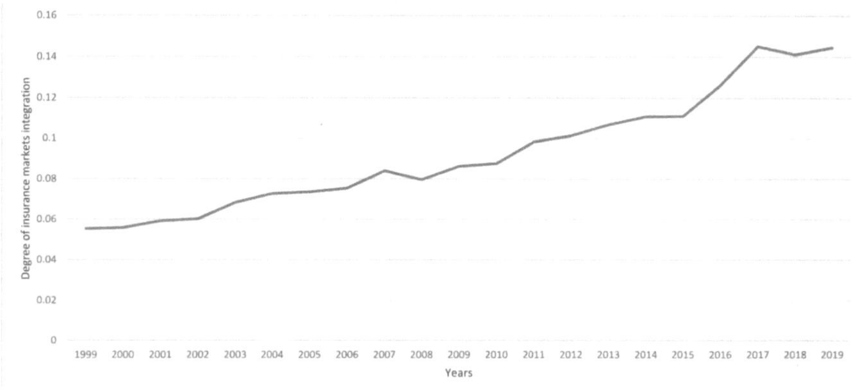

Figure 5.8 The degree of insurance market integration in the Euro area countries, measured with Q_g, in 1999–2019.

Source: The authors' calculation based on the OECD Statistics and Insurance Europe.

Table 5.5 The results of model estimation: Prais-Winsten, using 588 observations 1999–2019 (t = 21)

Specification	*Coefficient*	*Std. Error*	*t-ratio*	*p-value*	
Const	29.5157	0.566143	52.13	<0.0001	***
l_NCF	0.0773319	0.0231759	3.337	0.0039	***
l_IIg	0.161092	0.0492923	3.268	0.0045	***
l_Qg	0.285837	0.0268422	10.65	<0.0001	***

The statistics based on the rho-differenced data:

Sum squared resid	0.008105	S.E. of regression	0.021835
R-squared	0.950083	Adjusted R-squared	0.941274
F(3, 17)	36,597.19	P-value (F)	1.41e−32
Rho	−0.016112	Durbin-Watson	1.874919

The statistics based on the original data:

Mean dependent var	30.54666	S.D. dependent var	0.090062

Test for ARCH of order 1:

Null hypothesis: no ARCH effect is present

Test statistic: LM = 2.25472

with p-value = P(Chi-square (1) > 2.25472) = 0.133207

Test for normality of residual:

Null hypothesis: error is normally distributed

Test statistic: Chi-square (2) = 0.183819

with p-value = 0.912188

Source: The authors' own calculation using GRETL.

Dependent variable: L_GDP. Rho =0.292131

Explanation: *** The variable is significant at the significance level of 0.01; ** The variable is significant at the significance level of 0.05; * The variable is significant at the significance level of 0.1.

The results of model estimation for the Euro area

Engle-Granger cointegration test suggests the cointegration of the time series utilised in the model (cf. the test results below).

> *Augmented Dickey-Fuller test for uhat, testing down from 1 lags, criterion AIC*
> *sample size 20, unit-root null hypothesis: a = 1, test without constant*
> *including 0 lags of (1 – L)uhat*
> *model: (1 – L)y = (a – 1) × y(–1) + e*
> *estimated value of (a – 1): –0.589202*
> *test statistic: tau_ct(4) = –2.76086, critical value equal –1.95 with significance level 0.05*
> *p-value 0.754*
> *1st-order autocorrelation coeff. for e: 0.195*

The results in Table 5.6 show that all the variables are statistically significant with the exception of II_g, the normal distribution of the model's residuals is present and there is no ARCH effect, residue autocorrelation or heteroskedasticity.

The model explains 94% of the dependent variable's variance, which proves its good fit. The degree of insurance market integration, measured with Q_g, has a statistically significant effect on economic growth in the Euro area countries.

The most recent crisis (2008–2012) and insurance market integration in the Euro area

The analysis in Chapter 3 implies that the financial (monetary, capital, bond and interbank) market in the Euro area became fragmented during the financial and fiscal crisis (2008–2012), meaning their reduced integration.

The situation was completely different in the case of the insurance market in the Euro area. The financial and fiscal crisis did not contribute to a narrower degree of insurance market integration. On the contrary, the integration continued to increase. In fact, its degree measured with II_g did diminish in 2009, but was an inconsequential episode (see Figure 5.7).

Monetary policy – Impact on the degree of insurance market integration in the Euro area

The impact of the monetary policies in 2008–2019 on the degree of insurance market integration in the Euro area is examined.

To this end, the following models are designed:

$$\text{Model 1: } lnQg_{i,t} = a_1 + a_2 lnM3_{i,t} + a_3 M3_{i,t-1} + a_4 \Delta i3_{i,t} + u_{i,t} \quad (5.2)$$

Table 5.6 The results of model estimation: OLS, using 588 observations 1999–2019 (t = 21)

Specification	*Coefficient*	*Std. Error*	*t-ratio*	*p-value*	
Const	29.7744	0.285855	104.2	<0.0001	***
l_NCF	0.0416535	0.0120234	3.464	0.0030	***
l_IIg	−0.0319104	0.0441921	−0.7221	0.4801	
l_Qg	0.282560	0.0304347	9.284	<0.0001	***
Mean dependent var	30.26653	S.D. dependent var		0.074786	
Sum squared resid	0.006250	S.E. of regression		0.019175	
R-squared	0.944122	Adjusted R-squared		0.934262	
F(3, 17)	87.47671	P-value (F)		1.55e−10	
Log-likelihood	55.45837	Akaike criterion		−102.9167	
Schwarz criterion	−98.73864	Hannan-Quinn		−102.0100	
Rho	0.320804	Durbin-Watson		1.110915	
Breusch-Pagan test for heteroskedasticity:					
Null hypothesis:		heteroskedasticity not present			
Test statistic:		LM = 3.11845			
		with p-value = P(Chi-square (3) > 3.11845) = 0.373721			
White's test for heteroskedasticity:					
Null hypothesis:		heteroskedasticity not present			
Test statistic:		LM = 5.13801			
		with p-value = P(Chi-square (9) > 5.13801) = 0.822116			
LM test for autocorrelation up to order 1:					
Null hypothesis:		no autocorrelation			
Test statistic:		LMF = 1.89769			
		with p-value = P(F(1, 16) > 1.89769) = 0.187302			
Test for normality of residual:					
Null hypothesis:		error is normally distributed			
Test statistic:		Chi-square (2) = 1.57326			
		with p-value = 0.455377			
Test for ARCH of order 1:					
Null hypothesis:		no ARCH effect is present			
Test statistic:		LM = 1.01134			
		with p-value = P(Chi-square (1) > 1.01134) = 0.314582			

Source: The authors' own calculation with GRETL.

Dependent variable: L_GDP. HAC standard errors, bandwidth 2 (Bartlett kernel)

Explanation: *** The variable is significant at the significance level of 0.01; ** The variable is significant at the significance level of 0.05; * The variable is significant at the significance level of 0.1.

$$\text{Model 2: } lnIIg_{i,t} = a_1 + a_2 lnM3_{i,t} + a_3 M3_{i,t-1} + a_4 \Delta i3_{i,t} + u_{i.t} \quad (5.3)$$

where

Qg and *IIg* – the ratios of insurance market integration in the Euro area defined in Chapter 3,
M3 – money aggregate M3 in the Euro area,
I3 – Tyree-month rates of deposit interest in the interbank market in the Euro area,
Δ – operator of first differences,
ln – natural logarithm,
$u_{i,t}$ – joint random factor.

Annual data are used from the following databases: OECD Statistics, EIOPA, Eurostat, ORBIS, Insurance Europe and ECB.

The results of Engele-Granger cointegration test for model 1 (presented below) suggest the absence of a unit element and the cointegration of the time series utilised in this model.

Augmented Dickey-Fuller test for uhat, testing down from 1 lags, criterion AIC
sample size 11, unit-root null hypothesis: a = 1
test without constant, including 0 lags of (1 – L)uhat
model: (1 – L)y = (a – 1) × y(–1) + e
estimated value of (a – 1): –1.02845
test statistic: tau_ct(3) = –3.25367
p-value 0.4433
1st-order autocorrelation coeff. for e: –0.010

The cointegration of the time series applies to model 2 likewise (cf. the test results below).

Augmented Dickey-Fuller test for uhat, testing down from 1 lags, criterion AIC
sample size 10, unit-root null hypothesis: a = 1
test without constant, including one lag of (1 – L)uhat
model: (1 – L)y = (a – 1) × y(–1) + ··· + e
estimated value of (a – 1): –1.19209
test statistic: tau_ct(4) = –3.3424
asymptotic p-value 0.4144
1st-order autocorrelation coeff. for e: –0.045

The results of model 1 estimation [5.2] show that the autocorrelation of residuals or heteroskedasticity is absent, while the model residuals have a normal distribution. The model explains 95% of the dependent variable's variance (see Table 5.7).

The independent variables are statistically significant. The values of estimated coefficients of independent variables also point to a relatively strong and positive effect of monetary policy (the changes of interest rates and the money aggregate M3) on the variations to the degree of insurance market integration as measured with Q_g.

Table 5.7 The results of model 1 estimation: OLS, using 399 observations 2008–2019 (t = 12)

Specification	*Coefficient*	*Std. Error*	*t-ratio*	*p-value*	
Const	−59.4884	4.45357	−13.36	<0.0001	***
l_M3	0.0519115	0.0132077	3.930	0.0044	***
l_M3_1	1.86118	0.136967	13.59	<0.0001	***
d_i3	3.07131	0.564927	5.437	0.0006	***
Mean dependent var	−2.212454	S.D. dependent var		0.206519	
Sum squared resid	0.022006	S.E. of regression		0.052448	
R-squared	0.953094	Adjusted R-squared		0.935505	
F(3, 8)	280.3564	P-value (F)		1.93e−08	
Log-likelihood	20.78083	Akaike criterion		−33.56166	
Schwarz criterion	−31.62203	Hannan-Quinn		−34.27978	
Rho	0.042602	Durbin-Watson		1.800704	

Test for ARCH of order 1:
Null hypothesis: no ARCH effect is present
Test statistic: LM = 3.39805
with p-value = P(Chi-square (1) > 3.39805) = 0.0652735

White's test for heteroscedasticity:
Null hypothesis: heteroskedasticity not present
Test statistic: LM = 11.5268
with p-value = P(Chi-square (9) > 11.5268) = 0.241318

Test for normality of residual:
Null hypothesis: error is normally distributed
Test statistic: Chi-square (2) = 2.16732
with p-value = 0.338355

LM test for autocorrelation up to order 1:
Null hypothesis: no autocorrelation
Test statistic: LMF = 0.018706
with p-value = P(F(1, 7) > 0.018706) = 0.895063

Source: The authors' own calculation with using GRETL.

Dependent variable: L_Qg. HAC standard errors, bandwidth 1 (Bartlett kernel)

Explanation: *** The variable is significant at the significance level of 0.01; ** The variable is significant at the significance level of 0.05; * The variable is significant at the significance level of 0.1.

Table 5.8 The results of model 2 estimation: OLS, using 399 observations 2008–2019 (t = 12)

Specification	*Coefficient*	*Std. Error*	*t-ratio*	*p-value*	
Const	−22.1538	5.88682	−3.763	0.0055	***
l_M3	0.00855465	0.0150239	0.5694	0.5847	
l_M3_1	0.669005	0.183102	3.654	0.0065	***
d_i3	4.14352	1.04962	3.948	0.0043	***
Mean dependent var	−1.878525	S.D. dependent var		0.103301	
Sum squared resid	0.030743	S.E. of regression		0.061991	
R-squared	0.738096	Adjusted R-squared		0.639882	
F(3, 8)	26.51022	P-value (F)		0.000165	
Log-likelihood	18.77477	Akaike criterion		−29.54954	
Schwarz criterion	−27.60992	Hannan-Quinn		−30.26766	
Rho	0.281586	Durbin-Watson		1.215016	
Test for normality of residual:					
Null hypothesis:		error is normally distributed			
Test statistic:		Chi-square (2) = 1.47284 with p-value = 0.478824			
White's test for heteroskedasticity:					
Null hypothesis		heteroskedasticity not present			
Test statistic:		LM = 11.9451 with p-value = P(Chi-square (9) > 11.9451) = 0.216421			
LM test for autocorrelation up to order 1:					
Null hypothesis:		no autocorrelation			
Test statistic:		LMF = 0.805067 with p-value = P(F(1, 7) > 0.805067) = 0.399389			
Test for ARCH of order 1:					
Null hypothesis:		no ARCH effect is present			
Test statistic:		LM = 0.250661 with p-value = P(Chi-square (1) > 0.250661) = 0.61661			

Source: The authors' own calculation with GRETL.

Dependent variable: L_Iig. HAC standard errors, bandwidth 1 (Bartlett kernel)

Explanation: *** The variable is significant at the significance level of 0.01; ** The variable is significant at the significance level of 0.05; * The variable is significant at the significance level of 0.1.

The results of model 2 estimation [5.3] suggest that the autocorrelation of residuals and heteroskedasticity are absent, while the model residuals have a normal distribution. The model explains 73% of the variance of the dependent variable (see Table 5.8).

The independent variables are statistically significant. The values of estimated coefficients of independent variables also point to a relatively strong and positive effect of monetary policy (the changes of interest rates and the money aggregate M3) on the variations to the degree of insurance market integration as measured with II_g.

Conclusion

The empirical analysis in this chapter, based on statistical and econometric methods, suggests a few important conclusions regarding the integration of insurance markets in the EU and the Euro area.

The degree of insurance market integration measured by means of the ratios II_g and Q_g is quite high and tends to increase both across the EU and in the Euro area. Both the ratios of insurance market integration in the whole EU and in the Euro area are very similar, though somewhat higher in the Euro area than estimated for the entire EU.

There is a rather strong, positive and statistically significant impact of the variations of II_g and Q_g on economic growth in the EU countries. The situation in the Euro area is similar, although the effect of variable (ratio) II_g is statistically insignificant, whereas the impact of Q_g changes on the rate of economic growth is statistically significant and quite strong.

The financial and fiscal crisis in 2008–2012 failed to reduce the degree of insurance market integration, as opposed to that of other financial markets – the share, the treasury bond, monetary and interbank – as suggested in Chapter 3.

A significant positive impact of the ECB's monetary policy, measures with the changes of three-month interbank rates of interest and of the money aggregate, on the ratios of insurance market integration was present in the Euro area in 2008–2019.

Bibliography

AMECO Database, 2021. European Commission. Retrieved from https://ec.europa.eu/info/business-economy-euro/indicators-statistics/economic-databases/macro-economic-database-ameco/ameco-database_enon August 15, 2021.

ECB Statistical Data Warehouse, 2021. Retrieved fromhttps://sdw.ecb.europa.eu/on August 15, 2021.

EIOPA Database, 2021. Retrieved from https://www.eiopa.europa.eu/tools-and-data/statistics-and-risk-dashboards/insurance-statistics_en on July 15, 2021.

Eurostat Database, 2021. Retrieved from https://ec.europa.eu/eurostat/web/main/data/databaseon August 15, 2021.

Insurance Europe, 2021. Retrieved from https://www.insuranceeurope.eu/statisticson August 15, 2021.

OECD Statistics, 2021. Insurance Statistics. Retrieved from https://stats.oecd.orgon August 15, 2021.

ORBIS Database, 2021. Bureau van Dijk. A Moody's Analytics Company.

Index